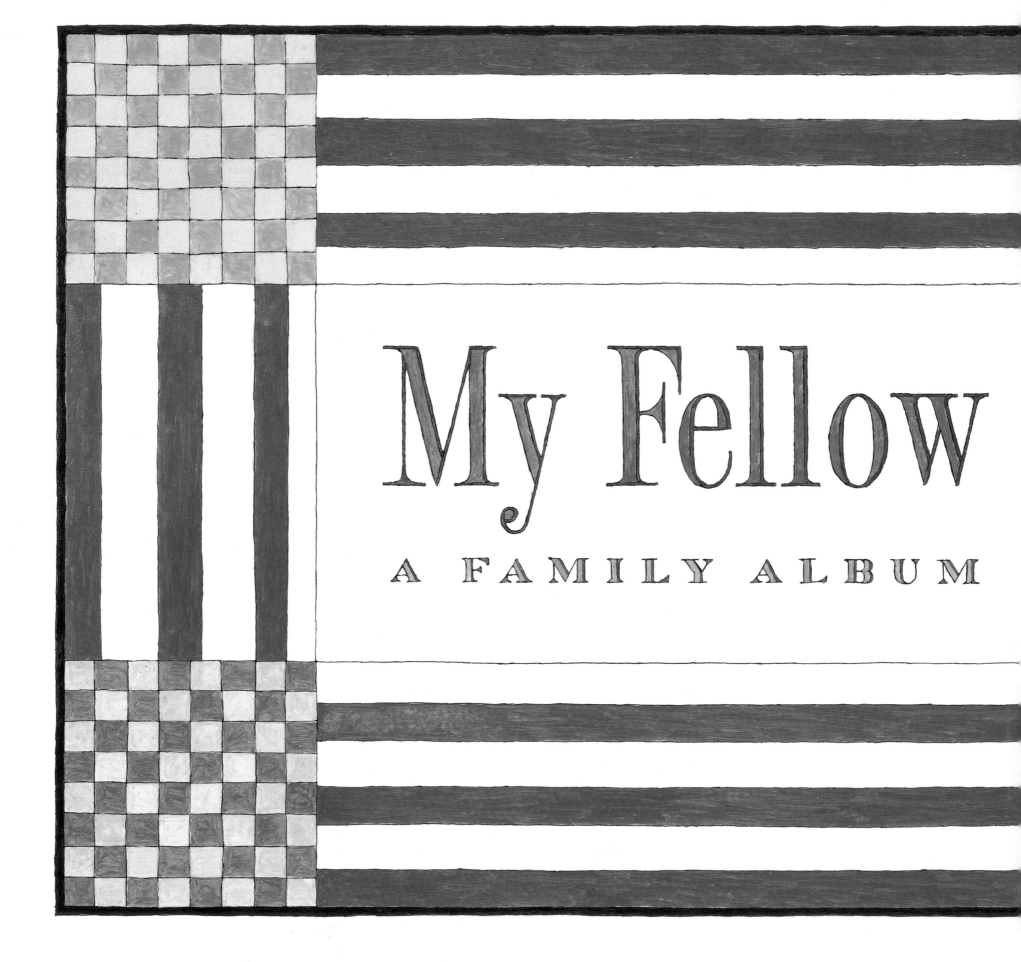

My Fellow

A FAMILY ALBUM

Americans

BY ALICE PROVENSEN

BROWNDEER PRESS
HARCOURT BRACE & COMPANY

San Diego   New York   London

TO LINDA ZUCKERMAN

FIDE ET FIDUCIA

SPECIAL THANKS TO

KAELIN CHAPPELL &

ROBIN CRUISE

A. P.

AND AGAIN AND ALWAYS FOR
KAREN, SEAN, JAMES, AND KELLY MITCHELL
BETH, ETHAN, ELISA, AND ERIK PROVENSEN
NINA AND JOSEF SOMMER • ALLELU AND JOHN KURTEN
MARIA AND ROBERT GOTTLIEB • DACIE AND WARREN KERSHAW

Requests for permission to make copies of any part of the work should be mailed to:
Permissions Department, Harcourt Brace & Company, 6277 Sea Harbor Drive,
Orlando, Florida 32887-6777.

Browndeer Press is a registered trademark of Harcourt Brace & Company.

Library of Congress Cataloging-in-Publication Data
Provensen, Alice.
My fellow Americans: a family album/Alice Provensen.
p. cm.
"Browndeer Press."
Summary: Tableaus and portraits of many of the individuals who have
influenced American history, culture, and character.
ISBN 0-15-276642-1
1. United States—History—Pictorial works.
[1. United States—History—Pictorial works.] I. Title
E178.5.P76   1995
973-dc20   95-15527

Printed in Singapore

First edition
A B C D E

The illustrations in this book were done in India ink and oil paint
on draughtsman's vellum.
The display type was hand-lettered by Alice Provensen.
The text type was set in Goudy Old Style.
Color separations by Bright Arts, Ltd., Singapore
Printed and bound by Tien Wah Press, Singapore
This book was printed with soya-based inks on Leykam recycled paper,
which contains more than 20 percent postconsumer waste and has a
total recycled content of at least 50 percent.
Production supervision by Warren Wallerstein and Ginger Boyer
Designed by Kaelin Chappell and Alice Provensen

AUTHOR'S NOTE

When I was young I fell in love with American place names—the towns and crossroads, rivers and battlefields whose names were left behind by Native Americans, the pilgrims, the immigrants: Chicago and Dakota, Providence and Missionary Ridge. There were the "new" names: New York, Bedford, and Hampshire; the saints' names: San Francisco, Diego, and Antonio. Their poetry filled me with awe and provided me with an interior landscape. They made me yearn to board the trains whose passenger cars were called Chautauqua or Steamboat Springs. I wanted to discover for myself our mysterious royalty, the *purple mountain majesties*. I dreamed of traveling the length of Route 66.

In the ensuing years I have seen much of this glorious landscape and have long since "populated" it with my fellow Americans—those people, born here or not, who are part of my education, my experience, and my recall. Americans touch me. They influence me. They have become my family.

Like all families, my American family has its rich uncles and poor relations, its atheists and believers, its scoundrels and bigots, its gifted and compassionate. Above all, these relatives are individuals, idiosyncratic and exceptional. In general I have been able to group them here by thought, by behavior, by métier. (Observations and reflections about them are included at the back of the book.) Pictured on the end sheets, front and back, are individuals who defy classification—Americans who are known for a single or unique act, invention, comment, work of art, tragedy, or who are somehow larger than life and have come to represent our myths and legends, our fantasies and our foibles.

Although some of the commentaries included beneath the pictures are contemporary, the Americans portrayed in these pages are no longer alive. There needed to be a limit to the length of my book; death provided it. Besides, since today's heroes may become tomorrow's fools, I thought it best not to include anyone still living. Those individuals who *are* included are my personal choices. Not all these Americans are honored in our national imagination, but they live in mine. They are the companions of my daily thoughts—a kind of natural resource; most important, they interest me.

I am aware that many distinguished Americans are not included here. Some have been omitted because they are from the more distant branches of my family—there are not many sports heroes, and judges, politicians, and philosophers are few. Many of our greatest scientists, entertainers, poets, writers, and athletes are still alive, which disqualifies them from inclusion. May they "live long and prosper."

—ALICE PROVENSEN

FRONT ENDPAPERS

Bartlett, Robert Abram (1875–1946)
Barton, Clara (1821–1912)
Bell, Alexander Graham (1847–1922)
Boone, Daniel (1734–1820)
Borglum, Gutzon (1867–1941)
Cody, Buffalo Bill (1846–1917)
Crockett, Davy (1786–1836)
Earhart, Amelia (1897–1937)
Garland, Judy (1922–1969)
Geisel, Theodor ("Dr. Seuss")
    (1904–1991)
Hale, Sarah (1788–1879)
Henson, Matthew Alexander
    (1866–1955)
Holmes, Oliver Wendell (1841–1935)
Jackson, Mahalia (1911–1972)
Jarvis, Gregory B. (1944–1986)
Jefferson, Thomas (1743–1826)
Kennedy, John F. (1917–1963)
Kent, Rockwell (1882–1971)
Lincoln, Abraham (1809–1865)
Malcolm X (1925–1965)
Marshall, John (1755–1835)
McAuliffe, Christa (1948–1986)
McNair, Ronald E. (1950–1986)
Mead, Margaret (1901–1978)
Miranda, Ernesto (1940–1976)
Monroe, Marilyn (1926–1962)
Moore, Clement C. (1779–1863)
Nation, Carry (1846–1911)
Oakley, Annie (1860–1926)
Onassis, Jacqueline Kennedy
    (1929–1994)
Onizuka, Ellison S. (1946–1986)
Peary, Robert Edwin (1856–1920)
Presley, Elvis (1935–1977)
Resnik, Judith A. (1949–1986)
Roebling, John A. (1806–1869)
Roosevelt, Theodore (1858–1919)
Scobee, Francis R. (1939–1986)
Smith, Kate (1907–1986)
Smith, Michael J. (1945–1986)
Sousa, John Philip (1845–1932)
Washington, George (1732–1799)
Webster, Daniel (1782–1852)
Wood, Grant (1891–1942)

**FREE SPIRITS
REBEL VOICES   10–11**

Bryan, William Jennings (1860–1925)
Darrow, Clarence (1857–1938)
Debs, Eugene V. (1855–1926)
Haywood, "Big Bill" (William)
    (1869–1928)
Scopes, John Thomas (1900–1970)
Thoreau, Henry David (1817–1862)

**PILGRIMS AND PURITANS
QUAKERS AND SHAKERS   12–13**

Bradford, William (1590–1657)
Lee, Mother Ann (1736–1784)
Massasoit (1580?–1661)

Penn, William (1644–1718)
Standish, Miles (1584?–1656)
Winslow, Edward (1595–1655)
Winthrop, John (1588–1649)

**MAVERICK MINISTERS
GUIDING LIGHTS   14–15**

Bethune, Mary McLeod (1875–1955)
Blavatsky, Madame (Helena Petrovna)
    (1831–1891)
Du Bois, W. E. B. (1868–1963)
Eddy, Mary Baker (1821–1910)
Eliot, John (1604–1690)
Jones, Sam ("Preacher") (1846–1906)
Judge, William Quan (1851–1896)
Mann, Horace (1796–1859)
McGuffey, William H. (1800–1873)
McPherson, Aimee Semple (1890–1944)
Olcott, Henry Steel (1832–1907)
Peale, Norman Vincent (1898–1993)
Ripley, George (1802–1880)
Sequoyah (1766?–1843)
Smith, Joseph (1805–1844)
Sullivan, Anne (1866–1936)
Sunday, Billy (William Ashley)
    (1862–1935)
Washington, Booker T. (1856–1915)
Webster, Noah (1758–1843)
Willard, Emma Hart (1787–1870)
Young, Brigham (1801–1877)

**THE IMPASSIONED FIGHTS
FOR FREEDOM AND
EQUAL RIGHTS   16–17**

Anthony, Susan B. (1820–1906)
Birney, James G. (1792–1857)
Bloomer, Amelia Jenks (1818–1894)
Brown, John (1800–1859)
Catt, Carrie Chapman (1859–1947)
Douglass, Frederick (1817–1895)
Garrison, William Lloyd (1805–1879)
Lundy, Benjamin (1789–1839)
Mott, James (1788–1868)
Mott, Lucretia (1793–1880)
Paul, Alice (1885–1977)
Phillips, Wendell (1811–1884)
Shaw, Anna Howard (1847–1919)
Stanton, Elizabeth Cady (1815–1902)
Stone, Lucy (1818–1893)
Stowe, Harriet Beecher (1811–1896)
Truth, Sojourner (1797–1883)
Tubman, Harriet (1820?–1913)

**WARRIORS AND
PATRIOTS   18–19**

Beauregard, Pierre Gustave Toutant de
    (1818–1893)
Bradley, Omar Nelson (1893–1981)
Corbin, Margaret (1751–1800?)
Crook, George (1829–1890)
Custer, George Armstrong (1839–1876)
Dewey, George (1837–1917)

Eisenhower, Dwight D. (1890–1969)
Franklin, Benjamin (1706–1790)
Gall (1840?–1894)
Grant, Ulysses S. (1822–1885)
Greene, Nathanael (1742–1786)
Hale, Nathan (1755–1776)
Hamilton, Alexander (1757?–1804)
Henry, Patrick (1736–1799)
Houston, Samuel (1793–1863)
Jones, John Paul (1747–1792)
Lawrence, James (1781–1813)
Lee, Robert E. (1807–1870)
Little Big Man (dates unknown)
MacArthur, Douglas (1880–1964)
Marshall, George Catlett (1880–1959)
Meade, George G. (1815–1872)
"Michigan" Bridget (Divers)
    (dates unknown)
Morris, Robert (1734–1806)
Nimitz, Chester William (1885–1966)
Paine, Thomas (1737–1809)
Patton, George Smith, Jr. (1885–1945)
Perry, Oliver Hazard (1785–1819)
Pershing, John Joseph (1860–1948)
Pickett, George E. (1825–1875)
Pitcher, Molly (Mary Ludwig Hays or
    Heis) (1754?–1832)
Rain in the Face (1835?–1905)
Revere, Paul (1735–1818)
Rickenbacker, Edward Vernon
    (1890–1973)
Scott, Winfield (1786–1866)
Shafter, William Rufus (1835–1906)
Shaw, Robert Gould (1837–1863)
Sheridan, Philip H. (1831–1888)
Sherman, William T. (1820–1891)
Sitting Bull (1831?–1890)
Taylor, George (1716–1781)
Washington, George (1732–1799)
York, Alvin Cullum (1887–1964)

**PICTORIAL HISTORIANS
THE FOURTH ESTATE   20–21**

Adams, Ansel (1902–1984)
Bly, Nellie (1867–1922)
Bourke-White, Margaret (1904–1971)
Brady, Mathew (1823?–1896)
Eastman, George (1854–1932)
Evans, Walker (1903–1975)
Gardner, Alexander (1821–1882)
Greeley, Horace (1811–1872)
Hearst, William Randolph (1863–1951)
Hine, Lewis (1874–1940)
La Guardia, Fiorello (1882–1947)
Luce, Henry R. (1898–1967)
McCarthy, Joseph R. (1908–1957)
Murrow, Edward R. (1908–1965)
Muybridge, Eadweard (1830–1904)
O'Sullivan, Timothy (1840–1882)
Pulitzer, Joseph (1847–1911)
Roosevelt, Eleanor (1884–1962)
Smith, Erwin E. (1888–1947)
Van Der Zee, James (1886–1983)

**THE MAGNETIC WEST:
PATHFINDERS, SETTLERS,
AND IMAGE MAKERS   22–23**

Bierstadt, Albert (1830–1902)
Bridger, Jim (1804–1881)
Catlin, George (1796–1872)
Clark, William (1770–1838)
Glidden, Joseph Farwell (1813–1906)
Grey, Zane (1875–1939)
Harte, Bret (1836–1902)
King, Henrietta (1832–1925)
King, Richard (1824–1885)
Lewis, Meriwether (1774–1809)
London, Jack (1876–1916)
Marshall, James Wilson (1810–1885)
Moran, Thomas (1837–1926)
Remington, Frederic (1861–1909)
Russell, Charles Marion (1864–1926)
Sacajawea (1786?–1884)
Wootton, "Uncle Dick" (Richens Lacy)
    (1816–1893)

**RADICAL REFORMERS AND
HUMANITARIANS   24–25**

Addams, Jane (1860–1935)
Bergh, Henry (1811–1888)
Riis, Jacob (1849–1914)
Sanger, Margaret (1883–1966)
Starr, Ellen Gates (1860–1940)

**MEGA-MILLIONAIRES:
INDUSTRIALISTS, FINANCIERS,
AND ROBBER BARONS   26–27**

Armour, Philip (1832–1901)
Astor, John Jacob (1763–1848)
Carnegie, Andrew (1835–1919)
Cooper, Peter (1791–1883)
Crocker, Charles (1822–1888)
Derby, Elias Hasket (1739–1799)
Drew, Dan (1797–1879)
Duke, James Buchanan (1856–1925)
Fisk, Jim (1834–1872)
Frick, Henry Clay (1849–1919)
Gould, Jay (1836–1892)
Havemeyer, Henry Osborne (1847–1907)
Hopkins, Mark (1802–1887)
Huntington, Collis (1821–1900)
Mellon, Andrew (1855–1937)
Morgan, J. Pierpont (1837–1913)
Pillsbury, Charles A. (1842–1899)
Rockefeller, John D. (1839–1937)
Stanford, Leland (1824–1893)
Swift, Gustavus F. (1839–1903)
Tarbell, Ida M. (1857–1944)
Vanderbilt, Cornelius (1794–1877)
Weyerhaeuser, Frederick (1834–1914)

**THE WOBBLIES AND
THE MINERS: SHOCK TROOPS
OF THE AFL-CIO   28–29**

Everest, Wesley (1890?–1919)
Flynn, Elizabeth Gurley (1890–1964)
Gompers, Samuel (1850–1924)

Haywood, "Big Bill" (William)
    (1869–1928)
Hill, Joe (1879–1915)
Jones, Mother (Mary Harris) (1830–1930)
Lewis, John L. (1880–1969)
Little, Frank H. (1879–1917)
Mitchell, John (1870–1919)

**THE PASTORAL PROTECTORS:
NATURALISTS AND
ECOLOGISTS   30–31**

Akeley, Carl Ethan (1864–1926)
Audubon, John James (1785–1851)
Bartram, William (1739–1823)
Burbank, Luther (1849–1926)
Burroughs, John (1837–1921)
Carson, Rachel (1907–1964)
Carver, George Washington (1864?–1943)
Chapman, John ("Johnny Appleseed")
    (1774–1845)
Ditmars, Raymond Lee (1876–1942)
Elliott, Henry Wood (1846–1930)
Gray, Asa (1810–1888)
Muir, John (1838–1914)
Olmsted, Frederick Law (1822–1903)
Richards, Ellen Swallow (1842–1911)
Stratton-Porter, Gene (1863–1924)

**WORKER IN THE VINEYARD
ECCENTRIC AUTOCRAT   32–33**

Chavez, Cesar (1927–1993)
Ford, Henry (1863–1947)

**EXPATRIATES:
AMERICANS ABROAD   34–35**

Baker, Josephine (1906–1975)
Baldwin, James (1924–1987)
Cassatt, Mary (1845?–1926)
Eliot, T. S. (1888–1965)
James, Henry (1843–1916)
Kelly, Grace (1929–1982)
Pound, Ezra (1885–1972)
Sargent, John Singer (1856–1925)
Simpson, Wallis Warfield (1896–1986)
Stein, Gertrude (1874–1946)
Whistler, James McNeill (1834–1903)

**WRITERS: FICTION,
HISTORY, ESSAYS, PLAYS,
AND CRITICISM   36–37**

Adams, Hannah (1755–1831)
Adams, Henry (1838–1918)
Alcott, Louisa May (1832–1888)
Alger, Horatio, Jr. (1832–1899)
Baum, L. Frank (1856–1919)
Brown, Margaret Wise (1910–1952)
Burnett, Frances Hodgson (1849–1924)
Cather, Willa (1873–1947)
Cooper, James Fenimore (1789–1851)
Crane, Stephen (1871–1900)
Dreiser, Theodore (1871–1945)
Emerson, Ralph Waldo (1803–1882)
Faulkner, William (1897–1962)
Fitzgerald, F. Scott (1896–1940)
Hawthorne, Nathaniel (1804–1864)

Hemingway, Ernest (1899–1961)
Henry, O. (William Sidney Porter) (1862–1910)
Howells, William Dean (1837–1920)
Irving, Washington (1783–1859)
Lewis, Sinclair (1885–1951)
Melville, Herman (1819–1891)
Mencken, H. L. (1880–1956)
Miller, Henry (1891–1980)
Odets, Clifford (1906–1963)
O'Neill, Eugene (1888–1953)
Parkman, Francis (1823–1893)
Prescott, William H. (1796–1859)
Steinbeck, John (1902–1968)
Twain, Mark (Samuel Langhorne Clemens) (1835–1910)
Warren, Mercy Otis (1728–1814)
Wharton, Edith (1862–1937)
Williams, Tennessee (1911–1983)
Wilson, Edmund (1895–1972)

POETS
POETS OF MOTION   38–39

Astaire, Fred (1899–1987)
Balanchine, George (1904–1983)
de Mille, Agnes (1908?–1993)
Dickinson, Emily (1830–1886)
Duncan, Isadora (1878?–1927)
Fuller, Loie (1869–1928)
Graham, Martha (1893?–1991)
Holm, Hanya (1893?–1992)
Hughes, Langston (1902–1967)
Humphrey, Doris (1895–1958)
Longfellow, Henry Wadsworth (1807–1882)
Lowell, Amy (1874–1925)
Lowell, James Russell (1819–1891)
Masters, Edgar Lee (1869–1950)
Moore, Marianne (1887–1972)
Poe, Edgar Allan (1809–1849)
Robinson, Bill ("Bojangles") (1878–1949)
Sandburg, Carl (1878–1967)
Shawn, Ted (1891–1972)
St. Denis, Ruth (1880?–1968)
Stevens, Wallace (1879–1955)
Weidman, Charles (1901–1975)
Whitman, Walt (1819–1892)
Whittier, John Greenleaf (1807–1892)
Williams, William Carlos (1883–1963)

AMERICAN ARCHITECTS:
THE SHAPES OF DEMOCRACY   40–41

Davis, Alexander Jackson (1803–1892)
Downing, Andrew Jackson (1815–1852)
Hunt, Richard M. (1828–1895)
Jefferson, Thomas (1743–1826)
McKim, Charles F. (1847–1909)
Mead, William R. (1846–1928)
Renwick, James (1818–1895)
Richardson, Henry Hobson (1838–1886)
Sullivan, Louis (1856–1924)
White, Stanford (1853–1906)
Wright, Frank Lloyd (1867–1959)

THE VISUAL ARTISTS   42–43

Bellows, George (1882–1925)
Benton, Thomas Hart (1889–1975)
Calder, Alexander (1898–1976)
Church, Frederick (1826–1900)
Cole, Thomas (1801–1848)
Copley, John Singleton (1738–1815)
Cropsey, Jasper Francis (1823–1900)
Curry, John Steuart (1897–1946)
Davies, Arthur B. (1862–1928)
Davis, Stuart (1894–1964)
Eakins, Thomas (1844–1916)
Feininger, Lyonel (1871–1956)
French, Daniel Chester (1850–1931)
Fulton, Robert (1765–1815)
Glackens, William (1870–1938)
Gropper, William (1897–1977)
Henri, Robert (1865–1929)
Hicks, Edward (1780–1849)
Hoffman, Malvina (1887–1966)
Homer, Winslow (1836–1910)
Hopper, Edward (1882–1967)
Inness, George (1825–1894)
Kane, John (1860–1934)
Kline, Franz (1910–1962)
Lawson, Ernest (1873–1939)
Luks, George (1867–1933)
Manship, Paul (1885–1966)
Morse, Samuel F. B. (1791–1872)
Moses, Grandma (nee Robertson, Anna Mary) (1860–1961)
Nevelson, Louise (1900–1988)
Noguchi, Isamu (1904–1988)
O'Keeffe, Georgia (1887–1986)
Peale, Charles Willson (1741–1827)
Pippin, Horace (1888–1946)
Pollock, Jackson (1912–1956)
Pratt, Matthew (1734–1805)
Prendergast, Maurice (1859–1924)
Rothko, Mark (1903–1970)
Ryder, Albert Pinkham (1847–1917)
Saint-Gaudens, Augustus (1848–1907)
Shahn, Ben (1898–1969)
Shinn, Everett (1876–1953)
Sloan, John (1871–1951)
Smith, David (1906–1965)
Stuart, Gilbert (1755–1828)
Trumbull, John (1756–1843)
Warhol, Andy (1928?–1987)
Zorach, William (1887–1966)

THE ENDURING ICONS:
ENTERTAINERS, IMPRESARIOS, AND SUPERSTARS   44–45

Ball, Lucille (1911–1989)
Bankhead, Tallulah (1903?–1968)
Bara, Theda (1890?–1955)
Barnum, P(hineas) T(aylor) (1810–1891)
Barrymore, Ethel (1879–1959)
Barrymore, John (1882–1942)
Barrymore, Lionel (1878–1954)
Belasco, David (1853–1931)
Benny, Jack (1894–1974)

Bogart, Humphrey (1899–1957)
Booth, Edwin (1833–1893)
Bow, Clara (1905–1965)
Capra, Frank (1897–1991)
Chaplin, Charlie (1889–1977)
Cooper, Gary (1901–1961)
Cornell, Katharine (1893?–1974)
Crawford, Joan (1908–1977)
Crosby, Bing (1904–1977)
Davis, Bette (1908–1989)
DeMille, Cecil B. (1881–1959)
Dietrich, Marlene (1901–1992)
Fairbanks, Douglas (1883–1939)
Fields, W. C. (1880–1946)
Fonda, Henry (1905–1982)
Fontanne, Lynn (1887–1983)
Gable, Clark (1901–1960)
Garbo, Greta (1905–1990)
Gilbert, John (1897?–1936)
Gish, Dorothy (1898–1968)
Gish, Lillian (1896–1993)
Grant, Cary (1904–1986)
Griffith, D(avid) W(ark) (1875–1948)
Hardy, Oliver (1892–1957)
Harlow, Jean (1911–1937)
Hart, W(illiam) S(urrey) (1870?–1946)
Hayes, Helen (1900–1993)
Hitchcock, Alfred (1899–1980)
Houdini, Harry (1874–1926)
Keaton, Buster (Joseph Francis) (1895–1966)
Kelly, Emmett (1898–1979)
Lassie
Laurel, Stan (1890–1965)
Lee, Gypsy Rose (1914–1970)
Lloyd, Harold (1893–1971)
Lunt, Alfred (1892?–1977)
Marx, Chico (Leonard) (1887?–1961)
Marx, Groucho (Julius) (1890?–1977)
Marx, Harpo (Arthur) (1888?–1964)
Merman, Ethel (1909–1984)
Nazimova, Alla (1879?–1945)
Pickford, Mary (1893–1979)
Rin Tin Tin
Robeson, Paul (1898–1976)
Rogers, Will (1879–1935)
Russell, Lillian (1861–1922)
Selznick, David O(liver) (1902–1965)
Sennett, Mack (1884–1960)
Swanson, Gloria (1899?–1983)
Tracy, Spencer (1900–1967)
Valentino, Rudolph (1895–1926)
Wayne, John (1907?–1979)
Welles, Orson (1915–1985)
West, Mae (1892?–1980)
White, Pearl (1889–1938)
Ziegfeld, Florenz (1867–1932)

COMPOSERS, CLASSY TUNESMITHS, AND ALL THAT JAZZ   46–47

Arlen, Harold (1905–1986)
Armstrong, Louis (1900–1971)
Barber, Samuel (1910–1981)

Basie, Count (William) (1904–1984)
Berlin, Irving (1888–1989)
Bernstein, Leonard (1918–1990)
Cohan, George M. (1878–1942)
Copland, Aaron (1900–1990)
Davis, Miles (1926–1991)
Ellington, Duke (Edward Kennedy) (1899–1974)
Foster, Stephen (1826–1864)
Gershwin, George (1898–1937)
Gershwin, Ira (1896–1983)
Gillespie, Dizzy (John Birks) (1917–1993)
Goodman, Benny (1909–1986)
Hammerstein, Oscar, II (1895–1960)
Hart, Lorenz (1895–1943)
Herbert, Victor (1859–1924)
Holiday, Billie (Eleanora) (1915–1959)
Ives, Charles (1874–1954)
Joplin, Scott (1868–1917)
Kern, Jerome (1885–1945)
MacDowell, Edward (1860–1908)
Miller, Glenn (1904–1944)
Monk, Thelonius (1917?–1982)
Parker, Charlie (1920–1955)
Porter, Cole (1891–1964)
Rodgers, Richard (1902–1979)
Romberg, Sigmund (1887–1951)
Smith, Bessie (1894?–1937)
Thomson, Virgil (1896–1989)
Waters, Ethel (1896–1977)

THE GREAT NATIONAL PASTIME: PACESETTERS AND GROUNDBREAKERS   48–49

Cartwright, Alexander Joy, Jr. (1820–1892)
Clemente, Roberto (1934–1972)
Cobb, Ty (1886–1961)
Creighton, Jim (1841–1862)
Ellard, George (1829–1916)
Gehrig, Lou (1903–1941)
Kelly, Mike ("King") (1857–1894)
Landis, Kenesaw Mountain (1866–1944)
Mathewson, Christy (1880–1925)
Paige, Satchel (1906–1982)
Rickey, Branch (1881–1965)
Robinson, Jackie (1919–1972)
Ruth, Babe (1895–1948)
Wright, Harry (1835–1895)

SCOUNDRELS AND THIEVES VILLAINS AND ROGUES   50–51

Arnold, Benedict (1741–1801)
Barrow, Clyde (1909–1934)
Bass, Sam (1851–1878)
"Billy the Kid" (William H. Bonney) (1859–1881)
Bolton, C. E. ("Black Bart") (1830–1917?)
Capone, Al ("Scarface") (1899–1947)
Cassidy, Butch (Robert Leroy Parker) (1866–1911?)
Cohn, Roy (1927–1986)
Dalton, Emmett (1871–1937)
Dalton, Grattan (1861–1892)
Dalton, Robert (1867?–1892)

Dillinger, John Herbert (1902?–1934)
Hoover, J. Edgar (1895–1972)
James, Frank (1843–1915)
James, Jesse (1847–1882)
Mather, Cotton (1663–1728)
McCarthy, Joseph R. (1908–1957)
Palmer, A. Mitchell (1872–1936)
Parker, Bonnie (1910–1934)
Smith, Jefferson R. ("The Skagway Skallywag") (1860–1898)
Starr, Belle (1848?–1889)
"Sundance Kid" (Harry Longbaugh) (1863–1911?)
Tweed, William Marcy (1823–1878)
Younger, Bob (1853–1889)
Younger, Cole (1844–1916)
Younger, Jim, (1848–1902)

INVENTING THE FUTURE:
THE INDIVIDUAL GENIUS   52–53

Edison, Thomas Alva (1847–1931)
Wright, Orville (1871–1948)
Wright, Wilbur (1867–1912)

INSPIRED PROPHETS
BOLD VISIONARIES   54–55

Fuller, R. Buckminster (1895–1983)
King, Martin Luther, Jr. (1929–1968)

BACK ENDPAPERS

Anderson, Marian (1902–1993)
Borden, Lizzie (1860–1927)
Burr, Aaron (1756–1836)
Cage, John (1912–1992)
Currier, Nathaniel (1813–1888)
Dean, James (1931–1955)
Disney, Walt (1901–1966)
Ellison, Ralph Waldo (1914–1994)
Feynman, Richard (1918–1988)
Flagg, James Montgomery (1877–1966)
Garvey, Marcus (1887–1940)
Guthrie, Woody (1912–1967)
Hamilton, Alexander (1755–1804)
Hancock, John (1737–1793)
Handy, W. C. (1873–1958)
Henson, Jim (1936–1990)
Ives, James Merritt (1824–1895)
Key, Francis Scott (1779–1843)
Lindbergh, Charles A., Jr. (1902–1974)
Marshall, Thurgood (1908–1993)
Mitchell, Margaret (1900–1949)
Palmer, Austin N. (1859–1927)
Payne, John Howard (1791–1852)
Pocahontas (1595?–1617)
Rockwell, Norman (1894–1978)
Roosevelt, Franklin D. (1882–1945)
Ross, Betsy (1752–1836)
Scott, Dred (1795?–1858)
Sullivan, John L. (1858–1918)
Taylor, Anna Edson (1858–1921)
Tecumseh (1766?–1813)
Thayer, Ernest Lawrence (1863–1940)
Tiffany, Louis Comfort (1848–1933)
Whitney, Eli (1765–1825)

FREE SPIRITS
HENRY DAVID THOREAU

THE HOUSE ON WALDEN POND, WHICH THOREAU BUILT BY HIMSELF AND LIVED IN FROM JULY 4, 1845, TO SEPTEMBER 6, 1847 CONCORD, MASS.

BUILDING COSTS: HOUSE, 10' W X 15' L	
TWO SECOND-HAND WINDOWS WITH GLASS	$2.43
REFUSE SHINGLES FOR ROOF AND SIDES	4.00
ONE THOUSAND OLD BRICK	4.00
HINGES AND SCREWS	0.14
TWO CASKS OF LIME	2.40
MANTLE-TREE IRON	0.15
TRANSPORTATION	1.40
BOARDS	8.03½
CHALK	0.01
LATCH	0.10
LATHS	1.25
NAILS	3.90
HAIR	0.31
IN ALL	$28.12½

POET · NATURALIST · SOCIAL CRITIC · REBEL

1854: WALDEN; OR, LIFE IN THE WOODS: ECONOMY · WHERE I LIVED, AND WHAT I LIVED FOR · READING · SOUNDS · SOLITUDE · VISITORS · THE BEAN-FIELD · THE VILLAGE · THE PONDS · BAKER FARM · HIGHER LAWS · BRUTE NEIGHBORS · HOUSE-WARMING · FORMER INHABITANTS; AND WINTER VISITORS · WINTER ANIMALS · THE POND IN WINTER · SPRING · CONCLUSION 1849: CIVIL DISOBEDIENCE 1859: A PLEA FOR CAPTAIN JOHN BROWN

"I dream of looking abroad summer and winter, with free gaze from some mountain-side…—I to be nature looking into nature with such easy sympathy as the blue-eyed grass in the meadow looking into the face of the sky."   —HENRY DAVID THOREAU

REBEL VOICES
CLARENCE DARROW

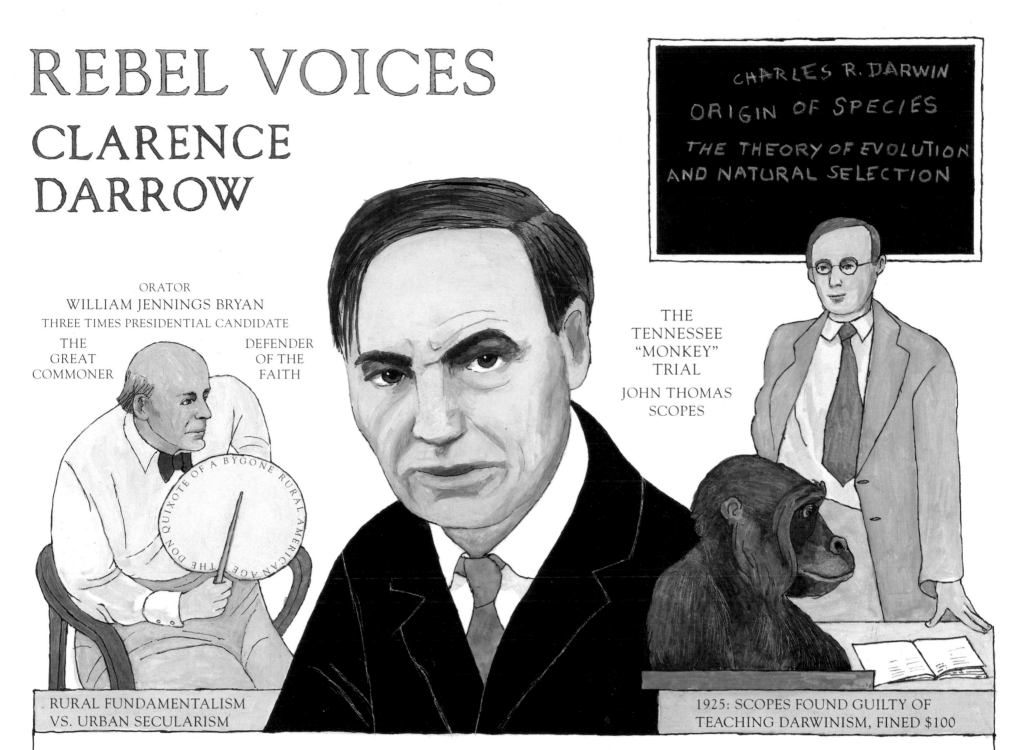

ORATOR
WILLIAM JENNINGS BRYAN
THREE TIMES PRESIDENTIAL CANDIDATE

THE
GREAT
COMMONER

DEFENDER
OF THE
FAITH

THE DON QUIXOTE OF A BYGONE RURAL AMERICA

CHARLES R. DARWIN
ORIGIN OF SPECIES
THE THEORY OF EVOLUTION
AND NATURAL SELECTION

THE
TENNESSEE
"MONKEY"
TRIAL

JOHN THOMAS
SCOPES

RURAL FUNDAMENTALISM
VS. URBAN SECULARISM

1925: SCOPES FOUND GUILTY OF
TEACHING DARWINISM, FINED $100

DEFENDER OF UNPOPULAR CAUSES

1894: DEFENDED EUGENE V. DEBS FROM IMPRISONMENT DURING THE PULLMAN STRIKE
1907: "BIG BILL" HAYWOOD ACCUSED OF THE MURDER OF THE GOVERNOR OF IDAHO; ACQUITTED AFTER AN 80-DAY TRIAL
1924: BROKE NEW LEGAL GROUND USING PSYCHOANALYTICAL DOCTRINES IN DEFENSE OF CONFESSED MURDERERS LEOPOLD & LOEB
DARROW DEFENDED OVER 100 PERSONS CHARGED WITH MURDER. NONE WAS EVER SENTENCED TO DEATH.

"I was dealing with life, with its fears, its aspirations and despairs. With me it was going to the foundation of motive and conduct and adjustments for human beings, instead of blindly talking hatred and vengeance and that subtle, indefinable quality that men call 'justice' and of which nothing really is known."
—CLARENCE DARROW

PILGRIMS AND PURITANS

MILES STANDISH
SOLDIER, DEFENDER OF THE COLONY AGAINST SUSPECT INDIANS

EDWARD WINSLOW
FOUNDER OF PLYMOUTH COLONY 1620

THE MAYFLOWER COMPACT
In the name of
We whose names
the loyall subj
soveraign Lo
by the grace of
Franc. and Irel
defender of the
haveing und
glorie of g

HISTORY OF PLIMMOUTH PLANTATION BY GOVERNOR Wᴹ BRADFORD

THE ARRIVAL OF THE ENGLISH IN THE LAND OF MASSASOIT, CHIEF OF THE WAMPANOAGS

THE MAYFLOWER COMPACT

JOHN WINTHROP
FIRST GOVERNOR OF THE MASSACHU-SETTS BAY COLONY 1630

THE PATERNAL DICTATOR

THE BAY PSALM BOOK
THE MUSIC OF THE PURITANS
FIRST BOOK PRINTED IN AMERICA
1640

ERECT ON THE UNENCUMBERED SOIL OF THE NEW WORLD A BIBLE COMMONWEALTH FREE OF THE CORRUPTION AND ADHESIONS OF THE OLD—THE FUNDAMENTAL AND CONTINUING ELEMENT IN THE AMERICAN EXPERIENCE

THE BIBLE COMMONWEALTH

"Being thus arived in good harbor and brought safe to land, they fell upon their knees and blessed the God of heaven, who had brought them over the vast and furious ocean, and delivered them from all the periles and miseries thereof, againe to set their feete on the firme and stable earth, their proper elemente."
—WILLIAM BRADFORD

QUAKERS AND SHAKERS

FOUNDER OF THE PEACEABLE KINGDOM AND THE CITY OF BROTHERLY LOVE

WILLIAM PENN
1681

THE "WALKING PURCHASE" OF 1686

THE DELAWARE INDIANS, THE MOST POWERFUL TRIBE OF ALL THE ALGONQUIANS, SIGN AN AGREEMENT WITH PENN THAT LASTED UNTIL PENN'S DEATH.

THE SOCIETY OF FRIENDS

FOUNDER OF THE FIRST SHAKER COMMUNITY IN AMERICA AT WATERVLIET, N.Y.

MOTHER ANN LEE
1776

SEPARATION FROM THE WORLD

THE ROUND BARN AT HANCOCK VILLAGE, MASS.

ECONOMIC, RACIAL, RELIGIOUS, AND SEXUAL EQUALITY
CELIBACY • COMMUNITY PROPERTY • PACIFISM
CONSECRATED WORK • OPEN CONFESSION OF SINS

THE MILLENNIAL CHURCH

"I had in my view Society, Assistance, Busy Commerce, Instruction of Youth, Government of Peoples manners, Conveniency of Religious Assembling, Encouragement of Mechanicks, distinct and beaten Roads, and it has answered in all those respects, I think, to an Universall Content." —WILLIAM PENN

MAVERICK MINISTERS

MENNONITES

THE PRINCIPLE OF NONRESISTANCE

GNADENAU, KANSAS

NORMAN VINCENT PEALE

THE POWER OF POSITIVE THINKING

THE OCCULT

SAM "PREACHER" JONES

ROOT HOG OR DIE POOR

APOSTLE TO THE INDIANS

JOHN ELIOT

THE HOLY BIBLE
TRANSLATED INTO THE ALGONQUIAN LANGUAGE BY JOHN ELIOT 1661–1663

MORMONISM

1848

THE NAUVOO TEMPLE BURNED

JOSEPH SMITH

BRIGHAM YOUNG

THE HIDING PLACE OF THE SECRET RECORDS REVEALED 1827

THEOSOPHY

MADAME BLAVATSKY

WILLIAM QUAN JUDGE

HENRY STEEL OLCOTT

EVANGELISM

BILLY SUNDAY

TRANSCENDENTALISM

GEORGE RIPLEY

ORGANIZER AND FOUNDER OF BROOK FARM, A COOPERATIVE COMMUNITY 1841

CHRISTIAN SCIENCE

MARY BAKER EDDY

HOLY BIBLE

SCIENCE AND HEALTH WITH A KEY TO THE SCRIPTURES

ANGELUS TEMPLE

AIMEE SEMPLE McPHERSON

WUTAPPESITTUKQUSSUN-NOOKWEHTUNKQUOH

MYSTIC UNION OF NATURE

SPIRITUAL HEALING

FOUR-SQUARE GOSPEL

"In what can the originality of any religious movement consist…? The force of personal faith, enthusiasm, and example, and above all the force of novelty, are always the prime suggestive agency."
—WILLIAM JAMES, *Philosopher and Psychologist*

GUIDING LIGHTS

EMMA HART WILLARD
PIONEER IN WOMEN'S EDUCATION

W. E. B. DU BOIS
AUTHOR AND EDITOR OF
THE CRISIS
NAACP MAGAZINE

ANNE SULLIVAN
TEACHER OF THE BLIND
INSPIRATION TO HELEN KELLER

SEQUOYAH
NATIVE AMERICAN SCHOLAR

SEQUOYAH'S SYLLABARY
TAUGHT THE CHEROKEE PEOPLE TO READ AND WRITE

BOOKER T. WASHINGTON
ORGANIZER AND FIRST PRESIDENT OF
TUSKEGEE INSTITUTE
1881

MARY McLEOD BETHUNE
FOUNDER OF DAYTONA NORMAL AND INDUSTRIAL INSTITUTE FOR NEGRO GIRLS
1904

"OLD GUFF"
PROFESSOR OF MORAL PHILOSOPHY

WILLIAM H. McGUFFEY

1836
THE FIRST ECLECTIC READER FOR CHILDREN

SECOND ECLECTIC READER 1836
THIRD ECLECTIC READER 1837
FOURTH ECLECTIC READER 1837
SIXTH ECLECTIC READER 1857
RHETORICAL GUIDE 1844

HORACE MANN
REVOLUTIONARY REFORMER OF "COMMON SCHOOLS"
- PROFESSIONALLY TRAINED TEACHERS
- COEDUCATION
- BETTER PAY
- IMPROVED SCHOOL-HOUSES

THE SPELLING BEE

1828
NOAH WEBSTER
LEXICOGRAPHER
THE AMERICAN DICTIONARY OF THE ENGLISH LANGUAGE

SPINGARN 1935 MEDAL

| PROPAEDEUTICS | PROFICIENCY | ERUDITION | ENLIGHTENMENT |

"What great hopes Americans have placed in formal education. What a stirring faith in children and in the possibility and power of universal intellectual improvement. And what a burden of idealism for the little places where education is actually attempted."
—TRACY KIDDER, *Writer*

THE IMPASSIONED FIGHTS FOR

ABOLITIONISTS

TRAIN FROM THE PATRIARCH DOMINION TO LIBERTYVILLE SEATS FREE IRRESPECTIVE OF COLOR

THE UNDERGROUND RAILROAD

JAMES MOTT

JAMES G. BIRNEY ★ FOR PRESIDENT ★ LIBERTY PARTY ★ 1840 & 1844 ★

"I NEVER LOST A PASSENGER." HARRIET TUBMAN

JOHN BROWN HANGED DEC. 2, 1859

LUCRETIA MOTT FOUNDER PHILADELPHIA FEMALE ANTI-SLAVERY SOCIETY

CHARLES TOWN, WEST VIRGINIA

UNCLE TOM'S CABIN HARRIET BEECHER STOWE

BENJAMIN LUNDY PUBLISHER OF THE GENIUS OF UNIVERSAL EMANCIPATION

WILLIAM LLOYD GARRISON PUBLISHER OF LIBERATOR

WENDELL PHILLIPS MASSACHUSETTS ANTI-SLAVERY SOCIETY

FREDERICK DOUGLASS PUBLISHER OF NORTH STAR

CAUTION! COLORED PEOPLE OF BOSTON BEWARE OF SLAVE CATCHERS AND KIDNAPPERS !!!

"I pity the poor in bondage that have none to help them; that is why I am here; not to gratify any personal animosity, revenge, or vindictive spirit. It is my sympathy with the oppressed and the wronged, that are as good as you, and as precious in the sight of God." —JOHN BROWN

FREEDOM AND EQUAL RIGHTS

WOMAN SUFFRAGISTS

JAILED FOR FREEDOM

PRISON SPECIAL

ERA

ALICE PAUL
FOUNDER
NATIONAL WOMAN'S PARTY

LUCY STONE

SUSAN B. ANTHONY

ELIZABETH CADY STANTON

SOJOURNER TRUTH

FAILURE IS IMPOSSIBLE

CARRIE CHAPMAN CATT

AMELIA JENKS BLOOMER

ANNA HOWARD SHAW

WOMAN'S JOURNAL — FOUNDED 1870

NATIONAL AMERICAN WOMAN SUFFRAGE ASSOCIATI

"MEN, THEIR RIGHTS, AND NOTHING MORE; WOMEN, THEIR RIGHTS, AND NOTHING LESS."
FIRST ISSUE
THE REVOLUTION
1868

WOMEN DEMAND THE RIGHT TO VOTE, TO OWN PROPERTY, TO WEAR "RATIONAL DRESS."

"Cautious, careful people, always casting about to preserve their reputation and social standing, never can bring about a reform."
—SUSAN B. ANTHONY

WARRIORS

THE SPANISH-AMERICAN WAR 1898: CUBA · MATAMOROS · THE MEXICAN WAR 1846–1848: PALO ALTO · THE ALAMO · THE TEXAS REVOLUTION 1836:

DEWEY

SHAFTER

TAYLOR

SCOTT

HOUSTON

"Don't give up the ship!"
JAMES LAWRENCE

"I have not yet begun to fight."
JOHN PAUL JONES

"We have met the enemy, and they are ours."
OLIVER HAZARD PERRY

HOPE

GEORGE WASHINGTON
FIRST IN WAR,
FIRST IN PEACE, AND
FIRST IN THE HEARTS
OF HIS COUNTRYMEN

MARGARET CORBIN AT FORT WASHINGTON

MOLLY PITCHER AT MONMOUTH

THE   UNKNOWN   SOLDIERS

SHERMAN   MEADE   SHERIDAN   SHAW   PICKETT   BEAUREGARD   LEE   JONES   GREENE   GRANT

"These are the times that try men's souls. The summer soldier and the sunshine patriot will, in this crisis, shrink from the service of their country; but he that stands it now, deserves the love and thanks of man

& PATRIOTS

ROBERT MORRIS

BENJAMIN FRANKLIN

PATRICK HENRY

ALEXANDER HAMILTON

PAUL REVERE

"I only regret that I have but one life to lose for my country."

NATHAN HALE

COMMON SENSE

THOMAS PAINE

1941–1945: PEARL HARBOR • MIDWAY • GUADALCANAL • ANZIO • NORMANDY • BATTLE OF THE BULGE • HIROSHIMA

EISENHOWER

PATTON

MARSHALL

BRADLEY

MacARTHUR

CUSTER RAIN IN THE FACE LITTLE BIG MAN GALL SITTING BULL CROOK RICKENBACKER YORK PERSHING NIMITZ

and woman. Tyranny, like hell, is not easily conquered; yet we have this consolation with us, that the harder the conflict, the more glorious the triumph."

—THOMAS PAINE

PICTORIAL HISTORIANS

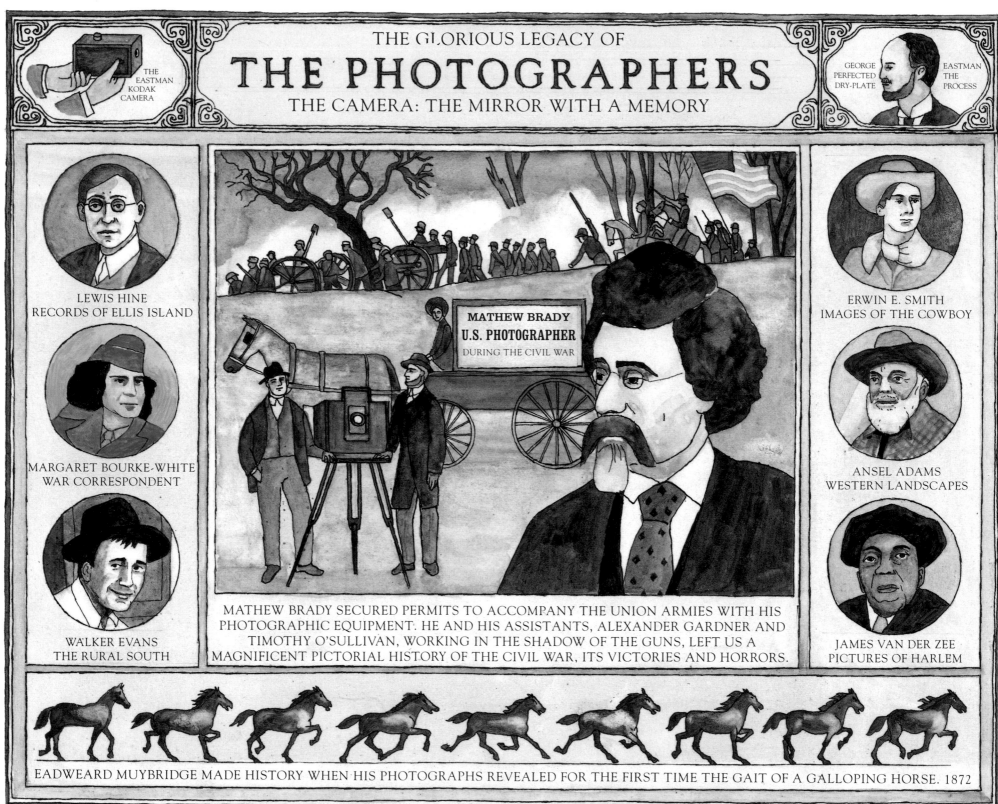

THE GLORIOUS LEGACY OF
THE PHOTOGRAPHERS
THE CAMERA: THE MIRROR WITH A MEMORY

THE EASTMAN KODAK CAMERA

GEORGE PERFECTED DRY-PLATE — EASTMAN THE PROCESS

LEWIS HINE
RECORDS OF ELLIS ISLAND

MARGARET BOURKE-WHITE
WAR CORRESPONDENT

WALKER EVANS
THE RURAL SOUTH

MATHEW BRADY
U.S. PHOTOGRAPHER
DURING THE CIVIL WAR

ERWIN E. SMITH
IMAGES OF THE COWBOY

ANSEL ADAMS
WESTERN LANDSCAPES

JAMES VAN DER ZEE
PICTURES OF HARLEM

MATHEW BRADY SECURED PERMITS TO ACCOMPANY THE UNION ARMIES WITH HIS PHOTOGRAPHIC EQUIPMENT. HE AND HIS ASSISTANTS, ALEXANDER GARDNER AND TIMOTHY O'SULLIVAN, WORKING IN THE SHADOW OF THE GUNS, LEFT US A MAGNIFICENT PICTORIAL HISTORY OF THE CIVIL WAR, ITS VICTORIES AND HORRORS.

EADWEARD MUYBRIDGE MADE HISTORY WHEN HIS PHOTOGRAPHS REVEALED FOR THE FIRST TIME THE GAIT OF A GALLOPING HORSE. 1872

"What is of greatest importance is to hold a moment, to record something so completely that those who see it will relive an equivalent of what has been expressed."
—ALFRED STIEGLITZ, *Photographer*

THE FOURTH ESTATE

NEWSPAPERS
MAGAZINES

AMERICANS IN THE NEWS
THE JOURNALISTS
PUBLISHERS • EDITORS • COLUMNISTS • REPORTERS

RADIO
TELEVISION

OWNER-PUBLISHER LEAVES PRIZE MONEY

CRUSADING EDITOR OF THE NEW YORK WORLD AND THE ST. LOUIS POST-DISPATCH NAMES PRIZES AFTER HIMSELF. 1902

HIS PAPERS HAD PHOTOS, CARTOONS, AGGRESSIVE NEWS COVERAGE, AND CRUSADES AGAINST CORRUPTION.

JOSEPH PULITZER

ESTABLISHES THE NATION'S MOST PRESTIGIOUS AWARDS FOR JOURNALISM AND OTHER FIELDS OF WRITING: FICTION, NONFICTION, POETRY, BIOGRAPHY, AND MUSIC COMPOSITION.

1936
AMERICA'S MOST INFLUENTIAL MAGAZINE PUBLISHER

HENRY R. LUCE

FOUNDER OF
TIME • LIFE • FORTUNE
SPORTS ILLUSTRATED
BUYS
ARCHITECTURAL FORUM

ON THE AIR

N.Y. MAYOR LA GUARDIA READS COMICS TO CHILDREN DURING NEWSPAPER STRIKE. 1942

GO WEST, YOUNG MAN!
FAMOUS EDITOR ADVISES AMERICAN YOUTH.

COFOUNDER OF THE NEW YORKER A WEEKLY JOURNAL DEVOTED TO LITERATURE, POLITICS, AND NEWS 1834

HORACE GREELEY

NEW YORK TRIBUNE
FIRST ISSUE: APRIL 10, 1841

FOR 125 YEARS THE TRIBUNE WAS ONE OF THE NATION'S GREATEST JOURNALISTIC INFLUENCES.

GREELEY ALONE SHAPED EDITORIAL POLICY.

SENSATIONAL POLICE NEWS AND OBJECTIONABLE ADVERTISING FOUND NO PLACE IN THE PAGES OF THE TRIBUNE.

LATE EVENING EDITION

Ironically, the quotation "Go west" is most often attributed to Greeley; him but was not originated with Some of Indiana the editor, the advice to of the Terre John Haute Express.

GREELEY'S OPINIONS WERE CONSIDERED AUTHORITATIVE ON ALMOST EVERY SUBJECT.

"YELLOW PRESS" OWNER BUILDS DREAM HOUSE

SAN SIMEON, CALIFORNIA   1919

HEARST CASTLE

FLAMBOYANT PICTURES, SHRIEKING TYPOGRAPHY, AND EARTHY MASS-APPEAL NEWS

EDWARD R. MURROW

VETERAN NEWSCASTER TAKES ON SENATOR JOSEPH McCARTHY. ACCUSES HIM OF USING HALF-TRUTHS TO

CONFUSE THE PUBLIC ABOUT THE THREAT OF COMMUNISM. 1954

SEE IT NOW

CBS

MURROW'S NAME REMAINS SYNONYMOUS WITH INTEGRITY AND EXCELLENCE.

AROUND THE WORLD IN A HOT-AIR BALLOON IN

72 DAYS!

JOURNALIST NELLIE BLY OUTDOES JULES VERNE'S PHILEAS FOGG. 1889–1890

"MY DAY"

PRESIDENT'S WIFE, ELEANOR ROOSEVELT, DESCRIBES HER ACTIVITIES IN HER DAILY COLUMN. 1936–1962

The New York Times
ESTABLISHED 1851

"All the News That's Fit to Print"

"Were it left to me to decide whether we should have a government without newspapers, or newspapers without a government, I should not hesitate a moment to prefer the latter." —THOMAS JEFFERSON, *President of the United States*

MERIWETHER LEWIS AND WILLIAM CLARK EXPLORE THE CONTINENT. 1803–1806

SACAJAWEA, A YOUNG SHOSHONE INTERPRETER AND GUIDE, POINTS OUT A PASS THROUGH THE ROCKY MOUNTAINS.

MOUNTAIN MAN

JIM BRIDGER
VERSATILE PIONEER

SHEEPMAN

"UNCLE DICK" WOOTTON
DROVE 9,000 SHEEP 1,600 MILES THROUGH INDIAN TERRITORY. 1852

FARMER

JOSEPH FARWELL GLIDDEN
PATENTED AND DEVELOPED BARBED WIRE. 1874

RICHARD AND HENRIETTA KING ON THEIR 600,000-ACRE STOCK RANCH, SANTA GERTRUDIS, TEXAS 1884

THE RUNNING W
∿∿
KING RANCH BRAND

THE PEERLESS LONGHORNS WITHSTAND HEAT, SURVIVE ON ARID LAND, AND GRAZE 15 MILES FROM WATER.

"The frontier is productive of individualism. . . . To the frontier the American intellect owes its striking characteristics. That coarseness and strength combined with acuteness and inquisitiveness; that practical, inventive turn of mind, quick to find expedients; that masterful grasp of material things, lacking in the artistic but powerful to effect great

PHOTOGRAPHER'S
ANNUAL HAYNES TOUR
PALACE
STUDIO CAR

DISCOVERED GOLD NEAR JOHN SUTTER'S MILL • 1848–1849 • THE CALIFORNIA GOLD RUSH •

JAMES WILSON MARSHALL

LEVI STRAUSS & CO.
COPPER RIVETED
SPRING BOTTOM PANTS

FARMS • HOMES • NORTHERN MISSOURI
Hannibal St. Joseph R R
OFFERS FOR SALE
500,000 ACRES
OF THE BEST
PRAIRIE • TIMBER • COAL
LANDS
IN THE WEST
LAND IS TO BE SOLD IN FORTY ACRE LOTS
ON 2 OR 10 YEARS CREDIT.
SECTIONAL MAPS AVAILABLE.

GEORGE CATLIN PAINTING
THE MANDAN CHIEF
FOUR BEARS

THE GUNS
THAT WON
THE WEST

WINCHESTER
REPEATING
RIFLE

FRONTIER
COLT
REVOLVER

SPINDLETOP
OIL WELL
USHERS IN
THE AGE OF
THE LONE
STAR
BILLIONAIRES

JANUARY 10,
1901, NEAR
BEAUMONT,
TEXAS

SPINNERS   OF YARNS

BRET HARTE   ZANE GREY   JACK LONDON
"THE LUCK OF   Riders of   THE CALL
ROARING   THE PURPLE   OF THE
CAMP"   SAGE   WILD

ALBERT   FREDERIC   THOMAS   CHARLES MARION
BIERSTADT   REMINGTON   MORAN   RUSSELL

PAINTINGS DID MUCH TO SPREAD THE ROMANCE OF THE WEST.
THESE ARTISTS, THROUGH THEIR UNTIRING LABOR,
PRESERVED ITS MYTHS AND ITS REALITIES.

PIONEERS CROSSING
THE PLAINS

ends; that restless, nervous energy; that dominant individualism, working for good and for evil, and withal that buoyancy and exuberance which comes with freedom—these are the traits of the frontier, or traits called out elsewhere because of the existence of the frontier."

—FREDERICK JACKSON TURNER, *Historian*

RADICAL REFORMERS

HENRY BERGH

"TO PLANT,
OR
REVIVE, THE
PRINCIPLE
OF MERCY
IN THE HUMAN
HEART..."

THE AMERICAN SOCIETY FOR THE ★ PREVENTION OF CRUELTY TO ANIMALS ★

1866

FOUNDER OF THE ASPCA

AN ANIMAL WELFARE SOCIETY CHARTERED JUST BEFORE PASSAGE OF THE NEW YORK ANIMAL PROTECTION ACT. BERGH, A TIRELESS PROTESTER AGAINST THE ABUSE OF ANIMALS, FOUGHT TO ABOLISH DOG AND RAT PITS, COCKFIGHTING, AND THE WRETCHED CONDITIONS UNDER WHICH WORKING ANIMALS LIVED AND FOOD ANIMALS WERE SLAUGHTERED. HE IS CREDITED WITH INVENTING THE CLAY PIGEON.

"This is a matter purely of conscience. It has no perplexing side issues.... It is a moral question in all its aspects.... It is a solemn recognition of that greatest attribute of the Almighty Ruler of the Universe, mercy, which if suspended in our case but for a single instant, would overwhelm and destroy us."   —HENRY BERGH

AND HUMANITARIANS

1889

POLICE
STATION
LODGERS
WAITING
TO BE
LET OUT

LITTLE
CARETAKER

CLINIC

JANE ADDAMS
SOCIAL WORKER

NOBEL LAUREATE

JACOB RIIS
INVESTIGATIVE REPORTER

MARGARET SANGER
NURSE

FOUNDER OF HULL HOUSE
COFOUNDER: ELLEN GATES STARR
PIONEERS OF AMERICA'S FIRST AND MOST IMPORTANT SETTLEMENT HOUSE, HALSTED STREET, CHICAGO, 1889 • BOOKS: THE SPIRIT OF YOUTH AND THE CITY STREETS, 1909; A NEW CONSCIENCE AND AN ANCIENT EVIL, 1912 • RECIPIENT OF THE NOBEL PEACE PRIZE, 1931 • A LEADER IN THE FEMINIST MOVEMENT

HOW THE OTHER HALF LIVES
1890

HOMELESS CHILDREN IN SLEEPING QUARTERS AT NIGHT

BIRTH CONTROL ADVOCATE
ORGANIZED THE FIRST AMERICAN BIRTH CONTROL CONFERENCE, 1923 • FOUNDER, AMERICAN BIRTH CONTROL LEAGUE • INDICTED UNDER THE COMSTOCK LAW FOR SENDING CONTRACEPTIVE INFORMATION THROUGH THE MAILS • JAILED FOR DISTRIBUTING BIRTH CONTROL LITERATURE • PRESIDENT, INTERNATIONAL PLANNED PARENTHOOD

"I believed it was my duty to place motherhood on a higher level than enslavement and accident. For these beliefs I was denounced, arrested, I was in and out of police courts and higher courts, indictments hung over my life for several years. But nothing could alter my beliefs. Because I saw these as truths, I stubbornly stuck to my convictions."   —MARGARET SANGER

THE 19TH CENTURY

MEGA-MILLIONAIRES IN

NEWPORT, RHODE ISLAND

"THE BREAKERS" MECCA FOR HIGH SOCIETY

PETER COOPER

THE ANOMALY OF THE GILDED AGE

MANUFACTURER · CIVIC AFFAIRS LEADER

TO SERVE MANKIND

AN HONEST MAN

IDA M. TARBELL

McCLURE'S MAGAZINE · WRITER · MUCKRAKER

HISTORY OF THE STANDARD OIL COMPANY 1904

TRUST BUSTER

THE SELF-INVENTED MONEY-MAKING MACHINES

ELIAS HASKET DERBY
SHIPPING

JOHN JACOB ASTOR CORNELIUS VANDERBILT J. PIERPONT MORGAN JOHN D. ROCKEFELLER

AMERICAN FUR CO. · N.Y. CENTRAL · U.S. STEEL · STANDARD OIL

FURS · RAILROADS · STEEL · PETROLEUM · BANKING

FREDERICK WEYERHAEUSER
LUMBER

"The production of wealth is not the work of any one man, and the acquisition of great fortunes is not possible without the co-operation of multitudes of men; and . . . therefore the individuals to whose lot these fortunes fall . . . should never lose sight of the fact that as they hold them by the will of society expressed in statute law, so they should administer them as trustees for the benefit of society as inculcated by moral law."
—PETER COOPER

ACQUISITION

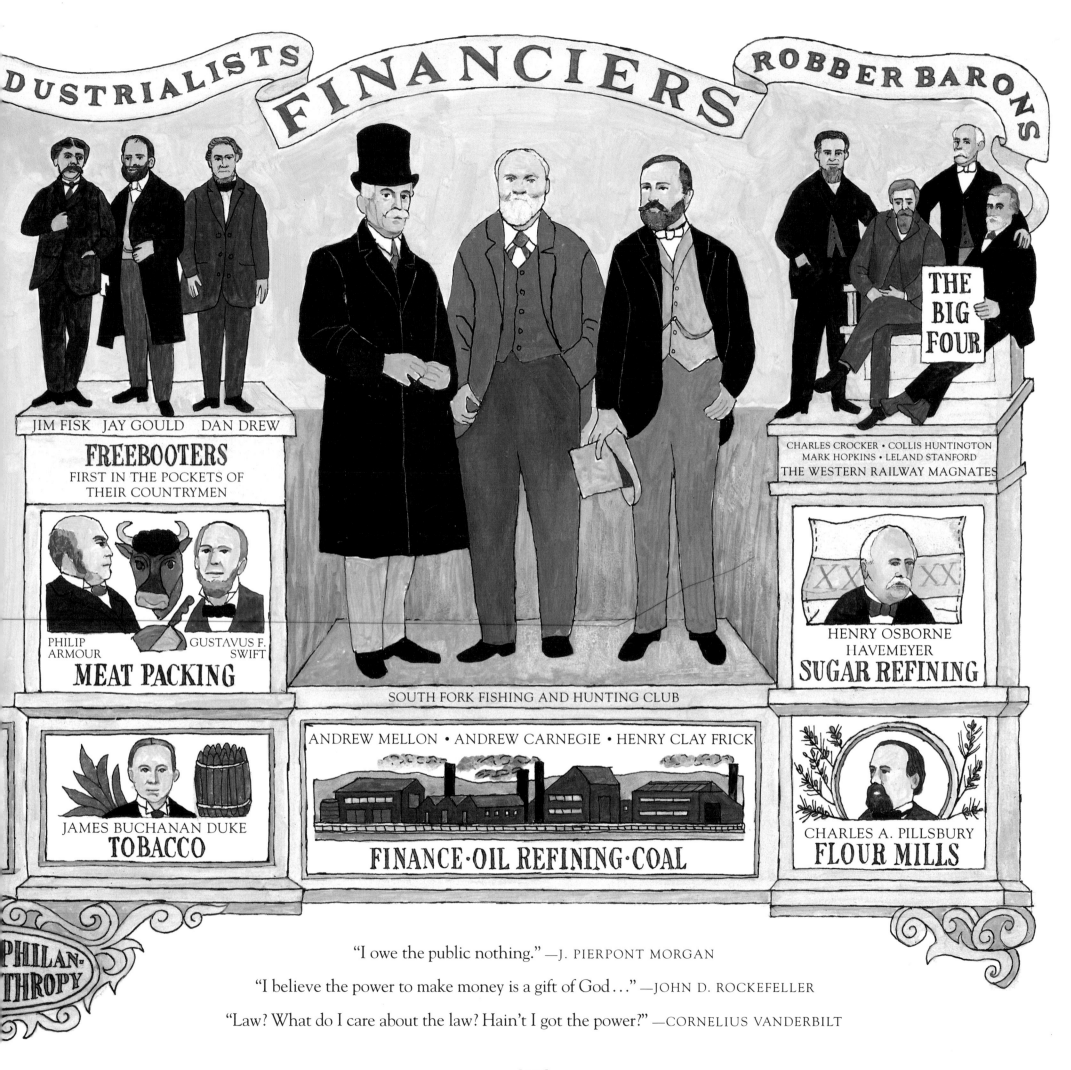

DUSTRIALISTS

FINANCIERS

ROBBER BARONS

JIM FISK JAY GOULD DAN DREW

FREEBOOTERS
FIRST IN THE POCKETS OF THEIR COUNTRYMEN

PHILIP ARMOUR   GUSTAVUS F. SWIFT

MEAT PACKING

JAMES BUCHANAN DUKE
TOBACCO

SOUTH FORK FISHING AND HUNTING CLUB

ANDREW MELLON • ANDREW CARNEGIE • HENRY CLAY FRICK

FINANCE · OIL REFINING · COAL

THE BIG FOUR

CHARLES CROCKER • COLLIS HUNTINGTON
MARK HOPKINS • LELAND STANFORD
THE WESTERN RAILWAY MAGNATES

HENRY OSBORNE HAVEMEYER
SUGAR REFINING

CHARLES A. PILLSBURY
FLOUR MILLS

PHILAN-
THROPY

"I owe the public nothing." —J. PIERPONT MORGAN

"I believe the power to make money is a gift of God…" —JOHN D. ROCKEFELLER

"Law? What do I care about the law? Hain't I got the power?" —CORNELIUS VANDERBILT

THE WOBBLIES AND THE MINERS:

1886 THE AMERICAN FEDERATION OF LABOR

SAMUEL GOMPERS
PRESIDENT 1896–1924

THE SKILLED CRAFT UNIONS OF THE AFL EXCLUDED THOUSANDS OF LABORERS IN MINES, MILLS, AND RAILROADS.

THE IWW IS COMING

JOIN THE **ONE BIG UNION**

WHAT TIME IS IT?

ORGANIZATION

TIME TO ORGANIZE

JOIN THE IWW

THE INDUSTRIAL WORKERS OF THE WORLD
ORGANIZED BY

THE PROLETARIAN JOAN OF ARC

ELIZABETH GURLEY FLYNN

"WE WANT BREAD AND ROSES TOO."

"BIG BILL" **WILLIAM HAYWOOD 1905**

1900–1920 THE YEARS OF DIRECT ACTION • THE WORKING-CLASS CRUSADE • BLACKLISTS • SCABS • LOCKOUTS •

• YELLOW-DOG CONTRACTS •

ARMED VIOLENCE • DYNAMITE • SABOTAGE • CONVICT LABOR • STRIKES •

THE "MARSEILLAISE" OF THE AMERICAN LABOR MOVEMENT

THE LITTLE RED SONG-BOOK

SOLIDARITY FOREVER

IWW MARTYRS
TO PROPERTY, PREJUDICE, AND THE LAW

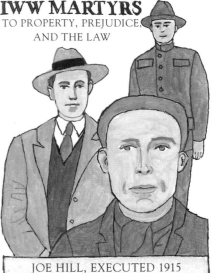

JOE HILL, EXECUTED 1915
FRANK H. LITTLE, LYNCHED 1917
WESLEY EVEREST, HANGED 1919

FELLOW WORKERS

Remember!
WE ARE IN HERE FOR YOU; YOU ARE OUT THERE FOR US.

"Ten thousand times has the labor movement stumbled and fallen and bruised itself, and risen again; been seized by the throat and choked into insensibility; enjoined by courts, assaulted by thugs, charged by the militia, shot down by regulars, traduced by the press, frowned upon by public opinion, deceived by politicians, threatened by priests, repudiated by renegades, preyed upon by grafters, infested by spies,

SHOCK TROOPS OF THE AFL-CIO

EPITAPH IN A COAL COUNTRY GRAVE-YARD:

"40 YEARS I WORKED WITH PICK AND DRILL. DOWN IN THE MINES AGAINST MY WILL. THE COAL KING'S SLAVE BUT NOW IT'S PASSED. THANKS BE TO GOD I AM FREE AT LAST."

R.I.P.

PRESIDENT OF THE **UMW** 1920–1960

JOHN L. LEWIS

THE **UNITED MINE WORKERS OF AMERICA**

THE FIRST MAJOR INDUSTRY-WIDE UNION 1890

MOTHER JONES

ORGANIZED WORKERS AT THE LATTIMER MINES, WHERE 26 ORGANIZERS HAD BEEN KILLED.

"The story of coal is always the same.... For a second's more sunlight, men must fight like tigers." —MARY HARRIS JONES

"THE COAL YOU DIG IS NOT SLAVISH OR POLISH OR IRISH COAL. IT'S JUST COAL."

1898–1908 **JOHN MITCHELL** FIRST PRESIDENT **UMW**

THE TRIAL OF ECONOMIC FEUDALISM 1902: THE GREAT ANTHRACITE STRIKE OF 114,700 WORKERS

1935 **CIO**

THE CONGRESS OF INDUSTRIAL ORGANIZATIONS

JOHN L. LEWIS, PRESIDENT

ORGANIZE THE UNORGANIZED

BREAKER BOYS AT WORK

"I felt that I was fighting for the boys, fighting a battle for innocent childhood." —JOHN MITCHELL

UNITED ELECTRICAL WORKERS · NAACP · ONE WORLD · UNITY · UNITED STATES CONFERENCE OF MAYORS · ACTORS EQUITY ASSO. · ONE · UNITED AUTO WORKERS · NEA · CIO AFL · ONE WORLD · UNITED STEEL WORKERS · ONE VOICE · ILGWU

SOLIDARITY WORKS

AFL-CIO · AUGUST 31, 1991 · WASHINGTON, D.C.

TENS OF THOUSANDS OF UNION MEMBERS JOIN CIVIL RIGHTS ACTIVISTS IN MARCH ON CAPITOL.

deserted by cowards, betrayed by traitors, bled by leeches, and sold out by leaders, but, notwithstanding all this, and all these, it is today the most vital and potential power this planet has ever known, and its historic mission of emancipating the workers of the world from the thralldom of the ages is as certain of ultimate realization as the setting of the sun."

—EUGENE V. DEBS, *Labor Leader*

HENRY WOOD ELLIOTT
GUARDIAN ANGEL OF THE FUR SEALS

JOHN CHAPMAN

JOHNNY APPLESEED

JOHN MUIR
JOHN OF THE MOUNTAIN

JOHN BURROUGHS
THE SAGE OF SLABSIDES

LUTHER BURBANK · HORTICULTURIST

WAKE ROBIN
FRESH FIELDS
BIRD & BOUGH

CONSERVATION CRUSADER
FOR NATIONAL PARKS

NATURIST · FRUIT GROWER
NATURE ESSAYIST

WILLIAM BARTRAM
NATURALIST

GENE STRATTON-PORTER
A GIRL OF THE LIMBERLOST

THE
LAST
PASSENGER
PIGEON
1914
MOUNTED AND PRESERVED IN THE SMITHSONIAN

BOTANIST · ASA GRAY · TAXONOMIST

"I would like to see all harmless wild things, but especially all birds, protected. . . .
When I hear of the destruction of a species I feel just as if all the works of some great writer had perished."
—THEODORE ROOSEVELT, *President of the United States*

RAYMOND LEE DITMARS
LEADING AUTHORITY ON SNAKES

RACHEL CARSON
PIONEER OF ECOLOGY

ELLEN SWALLOW RICHARDS
WATER · ANALYST
EUTHENIST · CHEMIST

PAINTER · JOHN JAMES AUDUBON · ORNITHOLOGIST

DDT
THE DEATH OF
FOURTEEN ROBINS

THE PERILS
OF
PESTICIDES

THE SEA AROUND US

SILENT SPRING

**THE
BIRDS OF AMERICA**
ONE OF THE GREATEST
ACHIEVEMENTS OF
AMERICAN ART

GEORGE WASHINGTON CARVER
AGRICULTURAL CHEMIST

THE THREATENED BALD EAGLE

FREDERICK LAW OLMSTED
PUBLIC PARKS DESIGNER

CARL ETHAN AKELEY
ANIMAL SCULPTURES IN MUSEUMS

"There are worlds on which life has never arisen. There are worlds that have been charred and ruined by cosmic catastrophes. We are fortunate: we are alive; we are powerful; the welfare of our civilization and our species is in our hands. If we do not speak for Earth, who will? If we are not committed to our own survival, who will be?"
—CARL SAGAN, *Astronomer*

WORKER IN THE VINEYARD

CESAR CHAVEZ

¡LA CAUSA! ¡VIVA!

¡LA HUELGA! ¡VIVA!

UNITED FARM WORKERS ORGANIZING COMMITTEE

"What the union will miss is Chavez's spiritual fire. . . . Self-sacrifice lay at the very heart of the devotion he inspired, and gave dignity and hope not only to the farmworkers but to every one of the Chicano people who saw for themselves what one brave man, indifferent to his own health and welfare, could accomplish."

—PETER MATTHIESSEN, *Writer*

ECCENTRIC AUTOCRAT

"THE GREATEST CREATION IN AUTOMOBILES EVER PLACED BEFORE A PEOPLE"

THE TIN LIZZIE

1908–1927
15 MILLION
SOLD

PRICED AT $290 IN 1924

"YOU CAN HAVE THE CAR IN ANY COLOR SO LONG AS IT'S BLACK."
20 HP 45 MPH

THE MODEL T

HENRY FORD
THE FLIVVER KING

THE REVOLUTION ON WHEELS TRANSFORMS THE FACE OF AMERICA

"The whole of the Ford plant seems stamped with its creator's qualities as few great industries are. You are aware of a queer combination of imaginative grandeur with cheapness, of meanness with magnificent will, of a North Western plainness and bleakness with a serviceable kind of distinction—the reflection of a personality that is itself a product of the cold winds, flat banks and monotony of those northern straits."
—EDMUND WILSON, *Social Critic*

EXPATRIATES
AMERICANS ABROAD

JAMES BALDWIN
WRITER

GRACE KELLY
PRINCESS OF MONACO

WALLIS WARFIELD SIMPSON
DUCHESS OF WINDSOR

EZRA POUND
POET
INDICTED FOR TREASON

T. S. ELIOT
POET
NOBEL PRIZE WINNER

"Even the most incorrigible maverick has to be born somewhere. He may leave the group that produced him—he may be forced to—but nothing will efface his origins, the marks of which he carries with him everywhere. I think it is important to know this and even find it a matter for rejoicing, as the strongest people do, regardless of their station." —JAMES BALDWIN

"There is something in this native land business and you cannot get away from it, in peace time you do not seem to notice it much particularly when you live in foreign parts but when there is a war and you are all alone and completely cut off from knowing about your country well then . . . it is your native land . . . it certainly is."

—GERTRUDE STEIN

WRITERS: FICTION · HISTORY

EUGENE O'NEILL

CLIFFORD ODETS

TENNESSEE WILLIAMS

EDMUND WILSON AXEL'S CASTLE 1931

THE ICEMAN COMETH 1946

WAITING FOR LEFTY 1935

CAT ON A HOT TIN ROOF 1955

ACT II

JAMES FENIMORE COOPER

HERMAN MELVILLE

W. H. P.

NATHANIEL HAWTHORNE THE SCARLET LETTER 1850

ESSAYS 1841–1844

RALPH WALDO EMERSON

HANNAH ADAMS A SUMMARY HISTORY OF NEW-ENGLAND 1799

BOSTON

HENRY ADAMS

MERCY OTIS WARREN TWO SATIRICAL PLAYS:

WASHINGTON IRVING RIP VAN WINKLE 1819

THE FIRST GREAT AMERICAN BOOK OF COMIC LITERATURE: DIEDRICH KNICKERBOCKER'S A HISTORY OF NEW YORK 1809

THE LAST OF THE MOHICANS

JAMES FENIMORE COOPER 1826

MOBY-DICK; OR, THE WHALE

HERMAN MELVILLE 1851

FRANCIS PARKMAN THE CALIFORNIA AND OREGON TRAIL 1849

HENRY ADAMS HISTORY OF THE UNITED STATES OF AMERICA DURING THE ADMINISTRATIONS OF THOMAS JEFFERSON AND JAMES MADISON 9 VOLS. 1889–1891

WILLIAM H. PRESCOTT HISTORY OF THE CONQUEST OF MEXICO 3 VOLS. 1843

THE ADULATEUR 1773 THE GROUP 1775

HISTORY OF THE RISE, PROGRESS, AND TERMINATION OF THE AMERICAN REVOLUTION 1805

"The aim of every artist is to arrest motion, which is life, by artificial means and hold it fixed so that a hundred years later, when a stranger looks at it, it moves again since it is life. Since man is mortal, the only immortality possible for him is to

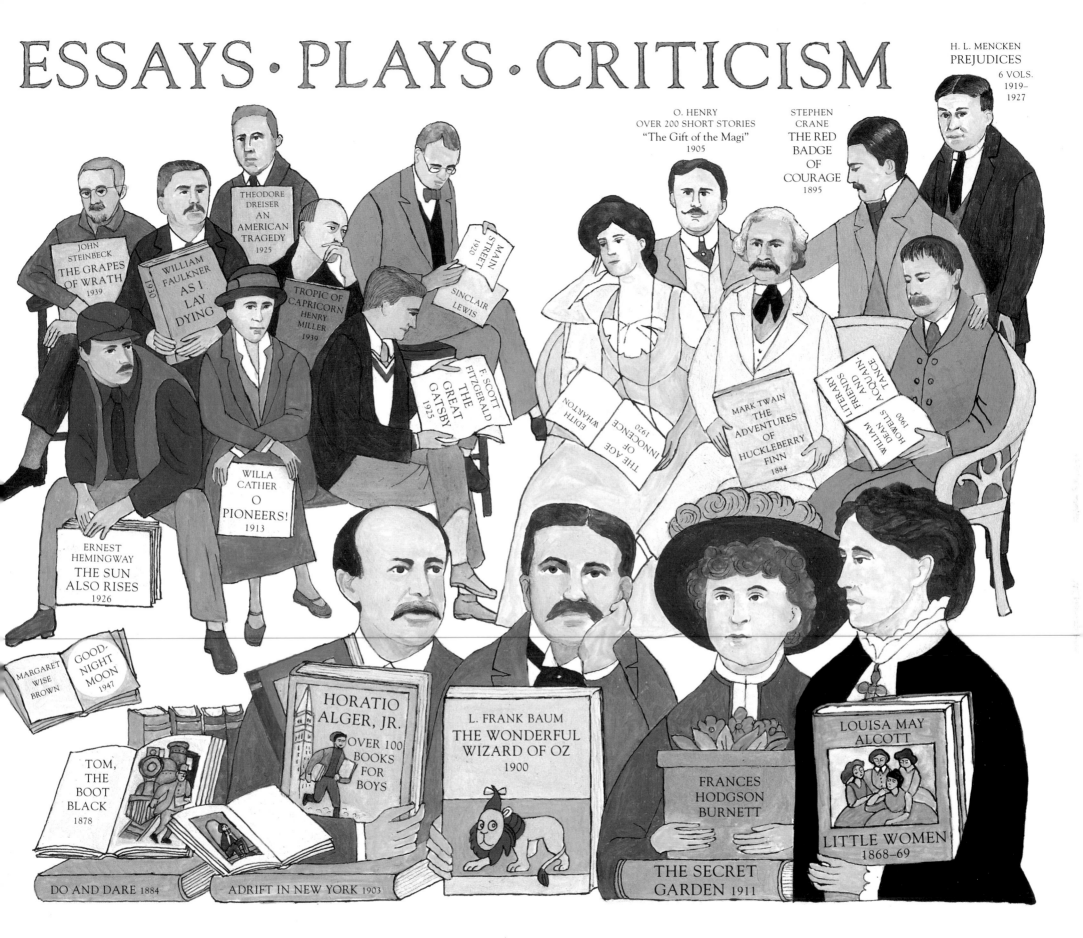

H. L. MENCKEN
PREJUDICES
6 VOLS.
1919–1927

O. HENRY
OVER 200 SHORT STORIES
"The Gift of the Magi"
1905

STEPHEN CRANE
THE RED BADGE OF COURAGE
1895

JOHN STEINBECK
THE GRAPES OF WRATH
1939

WILLIAM FAULKNER
AS I LAY DYING
1930

THEODORE DREISER
AN AMERICAN TRAGEDY
1925

TROPIC OF CAPRICORN
HENRY MILLER
1939

MAIN STREET
SINCLAIR LEWIS
1920

F. SCOTT FITZGERALD
THE GREAT GATSBY
1925

WILLA CATHER
O PIONEERS!
1913

THE AGE OF INNOCENCE
EDITH WHARTON
1920

MARK TWAIN
THE ADVENTURES OF HUCKLEBERRY FINN
1884

LITERARY FRIENDS AND ACQUAINTANCE
WILLIAM DEAN HOWELLS
1900

ERNEST HEMINGWAY
THE SUN ALSO RISES
1926

MARGARET WISE BROWN
GOODNIGHT MOON
1947

TOM, THE BOOT BLACK
1878

DO AND DARE 1884

HORATIO ALGER, JR.
OVER 100 BOOKS FOR BOYS

ADRIFT IN NEW YORK 1903

L. FRANK BAUM
THE WONDERFUL WIZARD OF OZ
1900

FRANCES HODGSON BURNETT

THE SECRET GARDEN 1911

LOUISA MAY ALCOTT
LITTLE WOMEN
1868–69

leave something behind him that is immortal since it will always move. This is the artist's way of scribbling 'Kilroy was here' on the wall of the final and irrevocable oblivion through which he must someday pass."   —WILLIAM FAULKNER

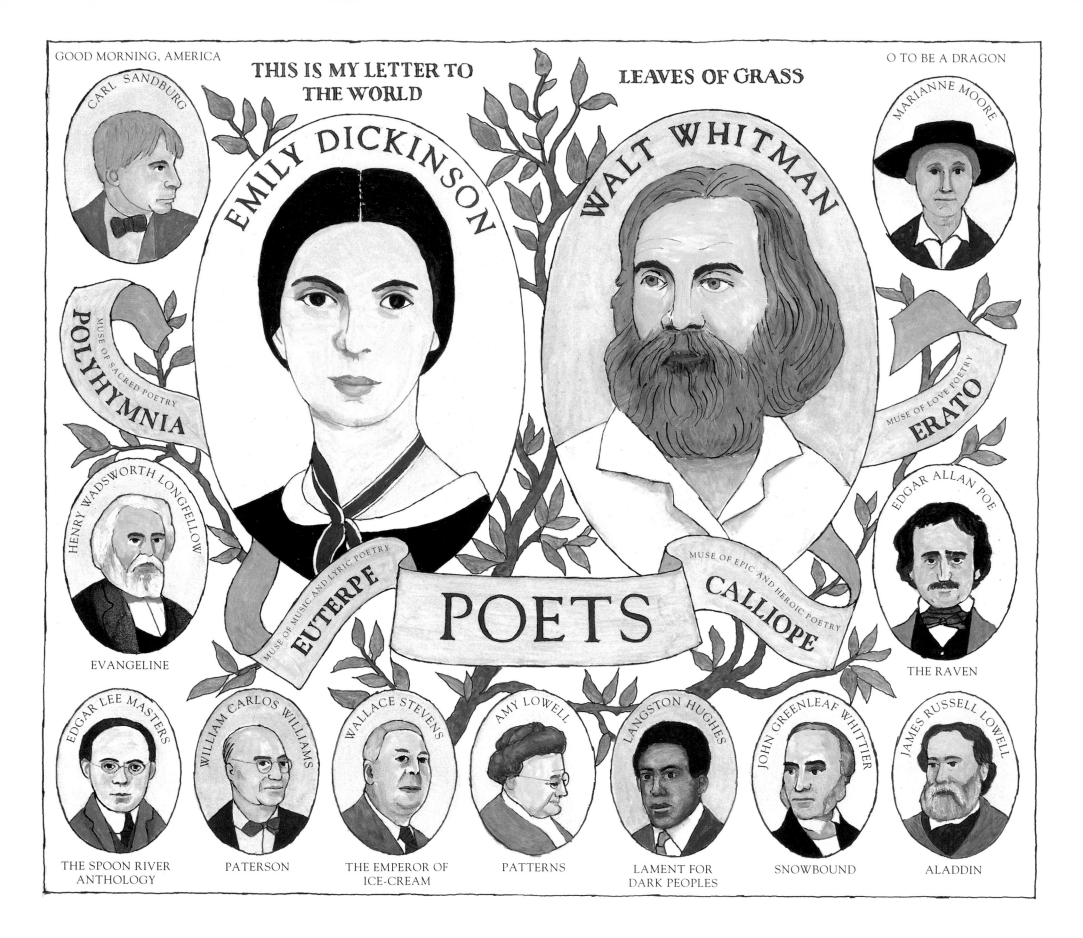

THIS IS MY LETTER TO THE WORLD

LEAVES OF GRASS

CARL SANDBURG

MARIANNE MOORE

EMILY DICKINSON

WALT WHITMAN

POLYHYMNIA
MUSE OF SACRED POETRY

ERATO
MUSE OF LOVE POETRY

HENRY WADSWORTH LONGFELLOW

EDGAR ALLAN POE

EUTERPE
MUSE OF MUSIC AND LYRIC POETRY

CALLIOPE
MUSE OF EPIC AND HEROIC POETRY

POETS

EVANGELINE

THE RAVEN

EDGAR LEE MASTERS

WILLIAM CARLOS WILLIAMS

WALLACE STEVENS

AMY LOWELL

LANGSTON HUGHES

JOHN GREENLEAF WHITTIER

JAMES RUSSELL LOWELL

THE SPOON RIVER
ANTHOLOGY

PATERSON

THE EMPEROR OF
ICE-CREAM

PATTERNS

LAMENT FOR
DARK PEOPLES

SNOWBOUND

ALADDIN

"The good poets have not generally sneered at the world of affairs. Some have, but many others have functioned well within that world. Yet the need and the right of all poets to detach themselves from the things of the world in order to pursue the things of the poetic trade have always been inseparable from their success as poets."

—JOHN CIARDI, *Poet*

MARTHA GRAHAM · FRED ASTAIRE · GEORGE BALANCHINE

AND THE EMERGENCE OF AN AMERICAN STYLE OF THEATER DANCING

MODERN DANCE

AN ORIGINAL
VOCABULARY
OF MOVEMENT

JAZZ
DANCING

AMERICA'S
GENUINE
ORIGINAL
FOLK ART

AGNES
DE MILLE

BILL "BOJANGLES"
ROBINSON

CHARLES WEIDMAN
DORIS HUMPHREY

CONTEM-
PORARY
BALLET

NEW
VARIATIONS
ON AN
ESTABLISHED
ART FORM

ISADORA DUNCAN · RUTH ST. DENIS
LOIE FULLER · HANYA HOLM · TED SHAWN

POETS OF MOTION

"Dancing differs from all other exercise.

"Sports require skill, coordination, and strength, but they are not dancing nor the stuff of dancing. Even when pleasing to watch, their real meaning lies in the practical results: the food caught, the game won, the record set.

"Dancing moves us. It excites us. It compels or persuades us. It reveals to us aspects of life and human emotion." —AGNES DE MILLE

AMERICAN ARCHITECTS:

CLASSIC REVIVAL

THOMAS JEFFERSON

STATE CAPITOL RICHMOND, VIRGINIA 1798

THOMAS JEFFERSON ARCHITECT

TIDEWATER CLASSICISM • SELF-MADE DESIGNERS

HENRY HOBSON RICHARDSON

RICHARDSONIAN ROMANESQUE

GOTHIC REVIVAL • GINGERBREAD

PATTERN BOOKS FOR HOUSES 1837

ALEXANDER JACKSON DAVIS • "RURAL RESIDENCES"

ROMANTIC

ANDREW JACKSON DOWNING

HERALD OF THE GOTHIC MANNER IN AMERICA

THE SMITHSONIAN INSTITUTION 1855

JAMES RENWICK ARCHITECT

A MASTERPIECE OF ROMANTIC ARCHITECTURE

"American architecture is composed, in the hundred, of 90 parts aberration, eight parts indifference, one part poverty, and one part Little Lord Fauntleroy. You can have the prescription filled at any architectural department store, or select architectural millinery establishment." —LOUIS SULLIVAN

THE SHAPES OF DEMOCRACY

RICHARD M. HUNT

SPECIALIZING IN MANSIONS FOR MILLIONAIRES

BEAUX ARTS

ORGANIC

CHARLES F. McKIM

WILLIAM R. MEAD

STANFORD WHITE

LOUIS SULLIVAN

FRANK LLOYD WRIGHT

THE CHICAGO SCHOOL

WASHINGTON SQUARE ARCH 1892

COLUMBIA UNIVERSITY LIBRARY 1897

McKIM, MEAD & WHITE ARCHITECTS NEW YORK CITY

A PANTHEON WITH A DIM READING ROOM

FORM EVER FOLLOWS FUNCTION

THE SOLOMON R. GUGGENHEIM MEMORIAL MUSEUM 1959

BUFFALO, NEW YORK

DARWIN D. MARTIN HOUSE 1904 • A MAJOR PRAIRIE-STYLE LANDMARK

"People will come to you and tell you what they want, and you will have to give them what they need. . . . I had to choose between honest arrogance and hypocritical humility. I chose honest arrogance, and have seen no reason to change."
—FRANK LLOYD WRIGHT

THE VISUAL ARTISTS

THE NATIVE TRIUMVIRATE

ALBERT PINKHAM RYDER

THOMAS EAKINS

WINSLOW HOMER

JOHN STEUART CURRY

THOMAS HART BENTON

NATIONALISM: REGIONAL REALISTS

POP ART

ANDY WARHOL

WILLIAM GROPPER

BEN SHAHN

SOCIAL REALISTS

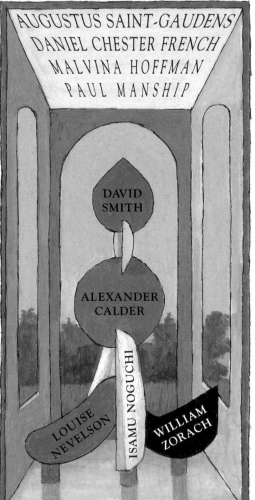

EDWARD HOPPER

AUGUSTUS SAINT-*GAUDENS*
DANIEL CHESTER *FRENCH*
MALVINA *HOFFMAN*
PAUL *MANSHIP*

DAVID SMITH

ALEXANDER CALDER

LOUISE NEVELSON

ISAMU NOGUCHI

WILLIAM ZORACH

SCULPTORS

BENJAMIN WEST'S AMERICAN PUPILS IN LONDON

SAMUEL F. B. MORSE

MATTHEW PRATT

CHARLES WILLSON PEALE

ROBERT FULTON

GILBERT STUART
FEDERAL ERA

JOHN TRUMBULL
GREATEST OF THE EARLY
ARTIST-PATRIOTS

JOHN SINGLETON COPLEY

THE FIRST AMERICAN-BORN
UNDISPUTED GENIUS

THE LINK WITH THE ENGLISH STYLE

NEOCLASSICISTS AND ROMANTICS

JACKSON POLLOCK

FRANZ KLINE

MARK ROTHKO

ABSTRACT EXPRESSIONISTS

"Art is not and cannot be a static thing. The public and the artist get bored with sameness, and the fatigued eye begins to look around for new exercises. Every art movement has within it individuals who are capable of moving on to the new ideas and new styles..." —JOHN K. HOWAT, *Art Curator*

THE ASHCAN SCHOOL

SLOAN

LUKS

GEORGE
INNESS

FREDERICK
CHURCH

JASPER
FRANCIS
CROPSEY

THOMAS
COLE

THE HUDSON RIVER SCHOOL

LYONEL FEININGER

STUART DAVIS

GEORGIA O'KEEFFE

DAVIES

GLACKENS

HENRI

LAWSON

PRENDERGAST

SHINN

ABSTRACT REALISTS

HORACE PIPPIN

THE
PRIMITIVES,
THE
SELF-TAUGHT,
AND
OUTSIDER
ART

JOHN
KANE

EDWARD HICKS

GRANDMA MOSES

THE ARMORY SHOW 1913
"THE EIGHT"

Front Row:
MAURICE PRENDERGAST
JOHN SLOAN
ROBERT HENRI
MiddleRow:
EVERETT SHINN
GEORGE LUKS
ERNEST LAWSON
Back Row:
WILLIAM GLACKENS
ARTHUR B. DAVIES

THE FORMATION OF
THE SOCIETY OF
INDEPENDENT
ARTISTS
1917

GEORGE BELLOWS

BELLOWS

"The purpose of art is always, ultimately, to give pleasure—though our
sensibilities may take time to catch up with the forms of pleasure that art
in a given time may offer."
—SUSAN SONTAG, *Cultural Historian*

PEARL WHITE THEDA BARA ALLA NAZIMOVA MACK SENNETT AND THE KEYSTONE KOPS CHICO, GROUCHO, AND HARPO MARX BUSTER KEATON JACK BENNY

EMMETT KELLY CHARLIE CHAPLIN OLIVER HARDY STAN LAUREL HAROLD LLOYD MAE WEST W. C. FIELDS JOHN, ETHEL, AND LIONEL BARRYMORE

LILLIAN AND DOROTHY GISH RUDOLPH VALENTINO JOHN GILBERT GRETA GARBO DOUGLAS FAIRBANKS MARY PICKFORD JEAN HARLOW CLARA BOW HUMPHREY BOGART

CARY GRANT PAUL ROBESON SPENCER TRACY CLARK GABLE HENRY FONDA JOHN WAYNE ETHEL MERMAN GARY COOPER W. S. HART RIN TIN TIN

HARRY HOUDINI EDWIN BOOTH MARLENE DIETRICH GLORIA SWANSON BETTE DAVIS JOAN CRAWFORD LILLIAN RUSSELL GYPSY ROSE LEE

ORSON WELLES WILL ROGERS DAVID BELASCO FLO ZIEGFELD P. T. BARNUM FRANK CAPRA CECIL B. DEMILLE DAVID O. SELZNICK D. W. GRIFFITH HELEN HAYES KATHARINE CORNELL

LUCILLE BALL

TALLULAH BANKHEAD

BING CROSBY

LASSIE

LYNN FONTANNE

ALFRED LUNT

THE ENDURING ICONS

ENTERTAINERS IMPRESARIOS AND SUPERSTARS

"I have constructed a little instrument which I call a Kinetoscope, with a nickel and slot attachment. Some 25 have been made, but [I] am very doubtful if there is any commercial feature in it."

—THOMAS ALVA EDISON, *Inventor*

COMPOSERS, CLASSY TUNESMITHS,

Stephen Foster • Charles Ives • Victor Herbert • Virgil Thomson
Samuel Barber • Aaron Copland • Edward MacDowell • Sigmund Romberg

IRVING BERLIN

LEONARD BERNSTEIN

JEROME KERN

HAROLD ARLEN

COLE PORTER

GEORGE M. COHAN

GEORGE GERSHWIN

WEST SIDE STORY

PORGY AND BESS
THREE PRELUDES
PIANO CONCERTO IN F
AN AMERICAN IN PARIS
RHAPSODY IN BLUE
OF THEE I SING

SCOTT JOPLIN

MAPLE LEAF RAG

PAL JOEY
JUMBO
ON YOUR TOES
OKLAHOMA

RICHARD RODGERS
SOUTH PACIFIC
CAROUSEL
ALLEGRO
THE KING AND I

LYRICISTS:
IRA GERSHWIN
LORENZ HART
OSCAR HAMMERSTEIN II

"With new sounds, new sonorities, new textures, dissonances, harmonies, rhythms, and that new objective approach, a great modern composer can use the same old-fashioned notes that music has always used, and use them in a fresh way."   —LEONARD BERNSTEIN

AND ALL THAT JAZZ

"Jazz is my adventure. I'm after new chords, new ways of syncopating, new figurations, new runs. How to use notes differently. That's it. Just using notes differently."
—THELONIUS MONK

THE GREAT NATIONAL PASTIME:

BABE RUTH

THE BEST-KNOWN, BEST-LOVED PLAYER
IN THE HISTORY OF BASEBALL •
IN HIS LIFETIME CAREER HE ESTABLISHED
OR EQUALED FIFTY-FOUR MAJOR LEAGUE RECORDS.

THE COLOSSUS OF CLOUT
THE BEHEMOTH OF BUST
THE SULTAN OF SWAT
THE BAMBINO

THE FATHER OF MODERN BASEBALL, ALEXANDER JOY CARTWRIGHT JR.,
DREW UP THE FIRST SET OF RULES. 1845

FIRST "MATCH GAME": THE KNICKERBOCKERS VS. THE NEW YORKS, PLAYED AT THE
ELYSIAN FIELD, HOBOKEN, NEW JERSEY 1846

THE EXCELSIORS: FIRST TEAM TO GO ON TOUR 1860 • JIM CREIGHTON,
PITCHER • FIRST AMATEUR STAR

THE ALL-BLACK PYTHIAN CLUB DENIED MEMBERSHIP IN THE
NATIONAL ASSOCIATION OF BASEBALL 1867

GEORGE ELLARD AND HARRY WRIGHT FORMED THE FIRST PROFESSIONAL TEAM:
THE CINCINNATI RED STOCKINGS. 1869

THE POLICE GAZETTE, THE FIRST DAILY NEWSPAPER TO FEATURE A SPORTS SECTION,
CREATED A GENRE OF BRILLIANT SPORTSWRITERS.

THE NATIONAL LEAGUE FORMED. 1876 • THE WESTERN LEAGUE BECAME
THE AMERICAN LEAGUE. 1899 • FIRST WORLD SERIES 1903

CHICAGO WHITE SOX SCANDAL 1919 • EIGHT PLAYERS BANNED BY
KENESAW MOUNTAIN LANDIS, COMMISSIONER 1920

THE BASEBALL HALL OF FAME OPENED
AT COOPERSTOWN, NEW YORK. 1939

ALL-AMERICAN GIRLS PROFESSIONAL
BASEBALL LEAGUE FORMED. 1943

LOUISVILLE SLUGGER
125

"Baseball is fathers and sons. . . . Baseball is fathers and sons playing catch, lazy
and murderous, wild and controlled, the profound archaic song of birth, growth,
age, and death. This diamond encloses what we are."
—DONALD HALL, *Poet*

PACESETTERS & GROUNDBREAKERS

JACKIE ROBINSON

BRANCH RICKEY, PRESIDENT, PART OWNER, AND GENERAL MANAGER OF THE BROOKLYN DODGERS, HAD THE COURAGE TO SIGN THE FIRST BLACK BASEBALL PLAYER TO A MAJOR LEAGUE TEAM. 1947 JACKIE ROBINSON HAD THE COURAGE TO TAKE THE JOB.

1947 FIRST ROOKIE OF THE YEAR
1949 MOST VALUABLE PLAYER AWARD,
MAJOR LEAGUE BATTING
CHAMPION

MIKE "KING" KELLY • THE ART OF THE SLIDE

CHRISTY MATHEWSON • THE CHRISTIAN GENTLEMAN

SATCHEL PAIGE • FOREVER YOUNG

LARRUPIN' LOU GEHRIG • THE IRON HORSE

MEAN-SPIRITED TY COBB • THE GEORGIA PEACH

ROBERTO CLEMENTE • FIRST HISPANIC HALL-OF-FAMER

"It breaks your heart. It is designed to break your heart. The game begins in the spring, when everything else begins again, and it blossoms in the summer, filling the afternoons and evenings, and then as soon as the chill rains come, it stops and leaves you to face the fall alone."
—A. BARTLETT GIAMATTI, *Commissioner of Baseball*

SCOUNDRELS AND THIEVES

TRAITOR

BENEDICT ARNOLD

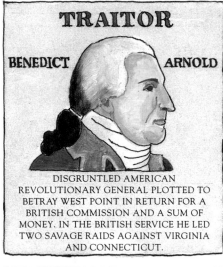

DISGRUNTLED AMERICAN REVOLUTIONARY GENERAL PLOTTED TO BETRAY WEST POINT IN RETURN FOR A BRITISH COMMISSION AND A SUM OF MONEY. IN THE BRITISH SERVICE HE LED TWO SAVAGE RAIDS AGAINST VIRGINIA AND CONNECTICUT.

ZEALOT

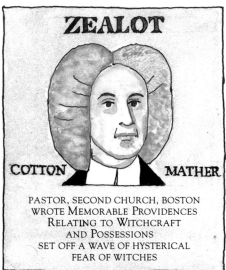

COTTON MATHER

PASTOR, SECOND CHURCH, BOSTON
WROTE MEMORABLE PROVIDENCES
RELATING TO WITCHCRAFT
AND POSSESSIONS
SET OFF A WAVE OF HYSTERICAL
FEAR OF WITCHES

EMBEZZLER

WILLIAM MARCY TWEED

BOSS OF TAMMANY HALL

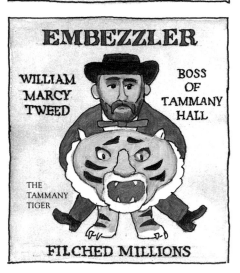

THE TAMMANY TIGER

FILCHED MILLIONS

HIGHWAYMAN

C. E. BOLTON

"BLACK BART"   THE RHYMING ROBBER

THE PO 8

MADE 27 SUCCESSFUL STAGECOACH HOLDUPS (OUT OF 28 TRIES), ALL WITH AN UNLOADED GUN.

$800 REWARD!

WILL BE PAID BY:
Wells, Fargo & Co.
for the arrest of the party who stole our
TREASURE BOX

ROMANTICIZED RUSTLERS & RENEGADES OUTLAWS, GUNMEN, & ROBBERS

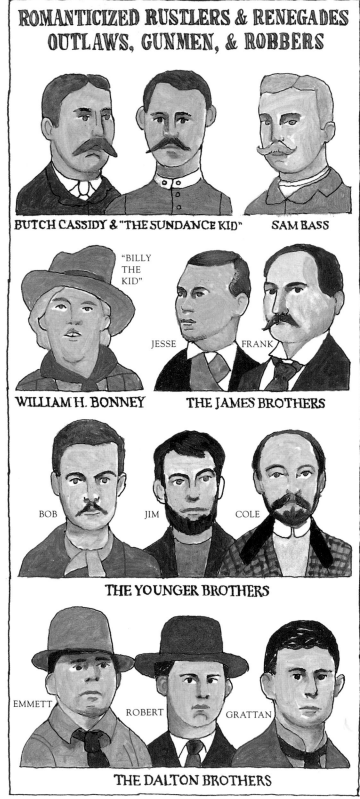

BUTCH CASSIDY & "THE SUNDANCE KID"   SAM BASS

"BILLY THE KID"

JESSE   FRANK

WILLIAM H. BONNEY   THE JAMES BROTHERS

BOB   JIM   COLE

THE YOUNGER BROTHERS

EMMETT   ROBERT   GRATTAN

THE DALTON BROTHERS

HORSE THIEF

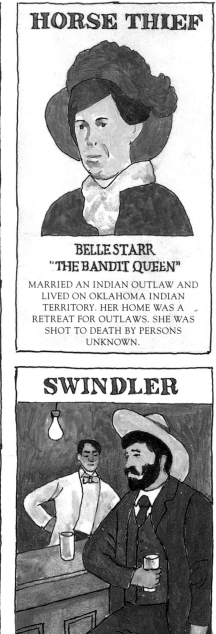

BELLE STARR
"THE BANDIT QUEEN"

MARRIED AN INDIAN OUTLAW AND LIVED ON OKLAHOMA INDIAN TERRITORY. HER HOME WAS A RETREAT FOR OUTLAWS. SHE WAS SHOT TO DEATH BY PERSONS UNKNOWN.

SWINDLER

JEFFERSON R. SMITH
"THE SKAGWAY SCALLYWAG"

A CROOKED ENTREPRENEUR IN THE KLONDIKE—THE MOST REMOTE PLACE IN THE LAND— HE RAN A FRAUDULENT LAND AND INFORMATION AGENCY.

"All who ever knew Billy will testify that his polite, cordial and gentlemanly bearing invited confidence and promised protection—the first of which he never betrayed and the latter he was never known to withhold. Those who knew him best will tell you that in his most savage and dangerous moods his face always wore a smile. He eat [sic] and laughed, drank and laughed, rode and laughed, fought and laughed, and killed and laughed."
—SHERIFF PAT GARRETT

VILLAINS AND ROGUES

PUBLIC ENEMY NO. 1

WANTED

JOHN HERBERT DILLINGER

$10,000.00

REWARD FOR THE CAPTURE OF PRISON ESCAPEE OR

$5,000.00

FOR INFORMATION LEADING TO THE ARREST OF SAME.

GANGSTER

"SCAR-FACE" AL CAPONE

90725

IMPLICATED IN BRUTAL MURDERS
ORGANIZED CRIME SYNDICATE
TERRORIZED CHICAGO IN THE
PROHIBITION ERA • ESTIMATED YEARLY
INCOME $105 MILLION

MOONSHINERS

THE FARMER'S DAUGHTERS
UNIDENTIFIED TEENAGERS
WORKING AT THEIR FATHER'S
STILL DURING PROHIBITION

HOODLUMS

BONNIE PARKER AND CLYDE BARROW, BANK ROBBERS

AMBUSHED BY A TEXAS RANGER AND
SHOT TO DEATH IN LOUISIANA

BIGOTS AND FANATICS, INSTIGATORS OF PUBLIC HYSTERIA

KU KLUX KLAN

ORGANIZED AT PULASKI, TENNESSEE 1866

A. MITCHELL PALMER

ATTORNEY GENERAL OF THE U.S.

THE PALMER RAIDS 3,000 ALIENS ARRESTED

SEN. JOSEPH R. McCARTHY

CHAIRMAN, SENATE PERMANENT COMMITTEE FOR INVESTIGATION

ROY COHN, CHIEF COUNSEL

FOUR TO FIVE MILLION MEMBERS AT
ITS PEAK IN MID-1920s

THE KKK: A SECRET SOCIETY
ORGANIZED TO MAINTAIN
"WHITE SUPREMACY" USING
TERROR, BURNING, AND
LYNCHING

"THE MAILED FIST OF THE AUTOCRATIC
TYRANT" • SLOGAN: SOS SHIP OR SHOOT!

McCARTHY, AFTER CENSURE BY THE SENATE, BECAME
EMOTIONALLY DISTURBED AND DIED OF ALCOHOLISM.

OUTRAGEOUS MISUSE OF FEDERAL POWER:
SECRECY • LACK OF SUBSTANTIATING EVIDENCE
CONFESSIONS PRODUCED BY COERCION
WANTON DISREGARD OF CIVIL RIGHTS • EXCESSIVE BAIL
MASS ARRESTS • VIOLENCE

HYPOCRITE

J. EDGAR HOOVER

CHIEF OF THE FBI

REWARD

DOG USED IN
PUBLICITY PHOTO TO
SOFTEN HOOVER'S IMAGE

DIRECTOR, FEDERAL BUREAU OF INVESTIGATION,
AN EFFECTIVE CRIME-FIGHTING ORGANIZATION

RULED THE FBI THROUGH USE OF
PROPAGANDA AND FEAR FOR HALF A
CENTURY • ENCOURAGED ILLEGAL
SNOOPING • MISUSED FEDERAL FUNDS • KEPT
SECRET FILES TO MANIPULATE POLITICIANS

"Everybody calls me a racketeer. I call myself a businessman. When I sell liquor, it's bootlegging. When my patrons serve it on a silver tray on Lake Shore Drive, it's hospitality." • "I make my money by supplying popular demand. If I break the law, my customers are as guilty as I am." • "Don't get the idea that I'm one of those goddamn radicals. Don't get the idea that I'm knocking the American system."
—AL CAPONE

INVENTING THE FUTURE:

THE INAUGURATION OF THE ELECTRICAL AGE

THOMAS ALVA EDISON

THE SELF-EDUCATED WIZARD OF PRACTICAL SCIENCE

THE FIRST PRACTICAL INCANDESCENT LIGHTBULB

1880

CALLED THE MOST USEFUL MAN IN AMERICA, EDISON FILED OVER 1,300 PATENTS. HIS KINETOSCOPE, AUTOMATIC TELEGRAPH SYSTEMS, ELECTRICAL GENERATORS, PHONOGRAPHS, AND STORAGE BATTERIES ALTERED OUR CIVILIZATION.

"There are two kinds of geniuses, the 'ordinary' and the 'magicians.' An ordinary genius is a fellow that you and I would be just as good as, if we were only many times better. There is no mystery as to how his mind works.... It is different with the magicians...the working of their minds is for all intents and purposes incomprehensible. Even after we understand what they have done, the process by which they have done it is completely dark."

—MARK KAC, *Mathematician*

THE INDIVIDUAL GENIUS

THE AGE OF FLIGHT

821,393. FLYING-MACHINE. Orville Wright and Wilbur Wright, Dayton, Ohio. Filed Mar. 23, 1903. Serial No. 149,220

To all whom it may concern:

Be it known that we, ORVILLE WRIGHT and WILBUR WRIGHT, citizens of the United States, residing in the city of Dayton, county of Montgomery, and State of Ohio, have invented certain new and useful Improvements in Flying-Machines, of which the following is a specification.

ORVILLE
AND
WILBUR
WRIGHT

THE FIRST SUSTAINED, CONTROLLED
AIRPLANE FLIGHT IN THE WORLD
KITTY HAWK, NORTH CAROLINA, DECEMBER 17, 1903

"Great scientific theories and great inventions are acts of creation and, like the composition of great music, the writing of great poetry, the painting of great pictures, they are the work of human beings of intense individuality, the very quality that the American republic was founded to enshrine. It is the potential that is latent in every American....its eventual release may well be America's greatest, most joyous victory."

—MITCHELL WILSON, *Physicist and Inventor*

INSPIRED PROPHETS

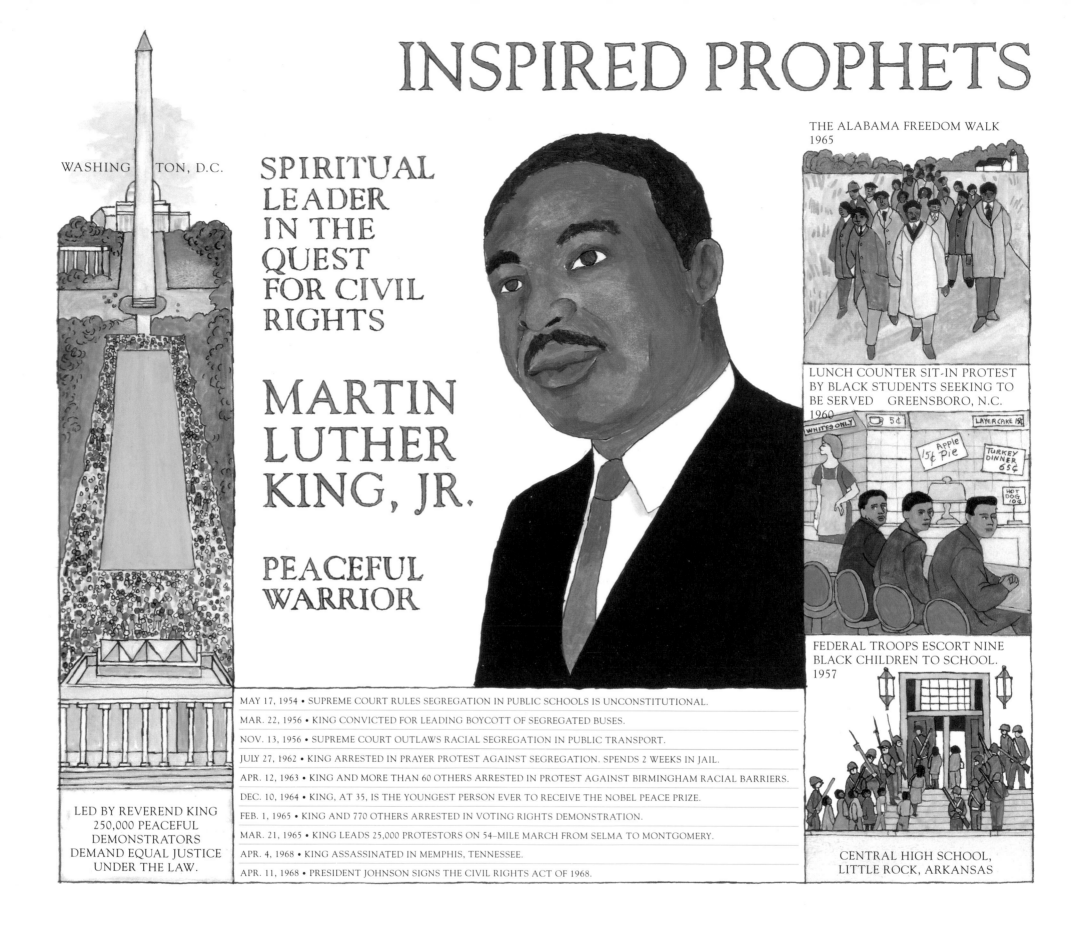

WASHINGTON, D.C.

SPIRITUAL
LEADER
IN THE
QUEST
FOR CIVIL
RIGHTS

MARTIN
LUTHER
KING, JR.

PEACEFUL
WARRIOR

THE ALABAMA FREEDOM WALK
1965

LUNCH COUNTER SIT-IN PROTEST
BY BLACK STUDENTS SEEKING TO
BE SERVED   GREENSBORO, N.C.
1960

WHITES ONLY   54   LAYER CAKE 15¢
15¢ Apple Pie   TURKEY DINNER 65¢   HOT DOG 10¢

FEDERAL TROOPS ESCORT NINE
BLACK CHILDREN TO SCHOOL.
1957

LED BY REVEREND KING
250,000 PEACEFUL
DEMONSTRATORS
DEMAND EQUAL JUSTICE
UNDER THE LAW.

MAY 17, 1954 • SUPREME COURT RULES SEGREGATION IN PUBLIC SCHOOLS IS UNCONSTITUTIONAL.

MAR. 22, 1956 • KING CONVICTED FOR LEADING BOYCOTT OF SEGREGATED BUSES.

NOV. 13, 1956 • SUPREME COURT OUTLAWS RACIAL SEGREGATION IN PUBLIC TRANSPORT.

JULY 27, 1962 • KING ARRESTED IN PRAYER PROTEST AGAINST SEGREGATION. SPENDS 2 WEEKS IN JAIL.

APR. 12, 1963 • KING AND MORE THAN 60 OTHERS ARRESTED IN PROTEST AGAINST BIRMINGHAM RACIAL BARRIERS.

DEC. 10, 1964 • KING, AT 35, IS THE YOUNGEST PERSON EVER TO RECEIVE THE NOBEL PEACE PRIZE.

FEB. 1, 1965 • KING AND 770 OTHERS ARRESTED IN VOTING RIGHTS DEMONSTRATION.

MAR. 21, 1965 • KING LEADS 25,000 PROTESTORS ON 54–MILE MARCH FROM SELMA TO MONTGOMERY.

APR. 4, 1968 • KING ASSASSINATED IN MEMPHIS, TENNESSEE.

APR. 11, 1968 • PRESIDENT JOHNSON SIGNS THE CIVIL RIGHTS ACT OF 1968.

CENTRAL HIGH SCHOOL,
LITTLE ROCK, ARKANSAS

"Through our scientific genius, we have made of the world a neighborhood; now through our moral and spiritual genius we must make of it a
brotherhood."
—MARTIN LUTHER KING, JR.

BOLD VISIONARIES

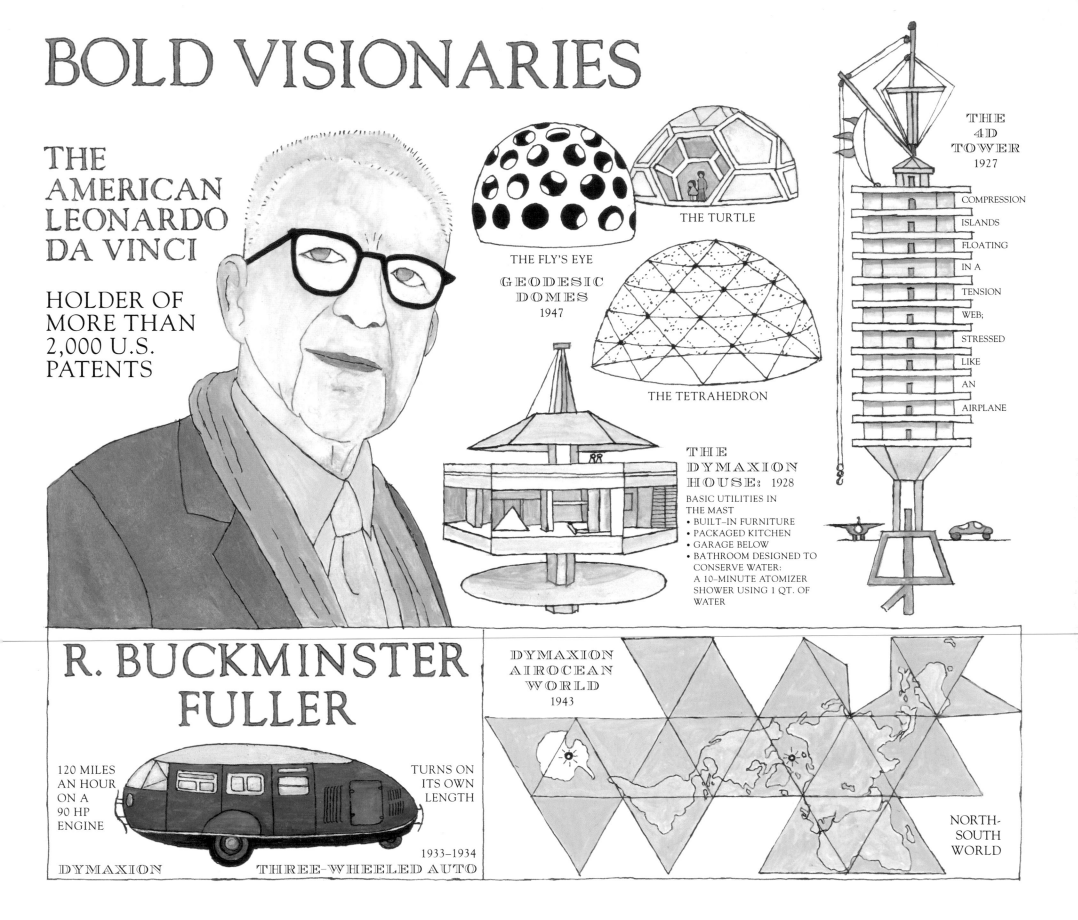

THE AMERICAN LEONARDO DA VINCI

HOLDER OF MORE THAN 2,000 U.S. PATENTS

THE FLY'S EYE

THE TURTLE

GEODESIC DOMES 1947

THE TETRAHEDRON

THE DYMAXION HOUSE: 1928
BASIC UTILITIES IN THE MAST
• BUILT–IN FURNITURE
• PACKAGED KITCHEN
• GARAGE BELOW
• BATHROOM DESIGNED TO CONSERVE WATER: A 10–MINUTE ATOMIZER SHOWER USING 1 QT. OF WATER

THE 4D TOWER 1927

COMPRESSION ISLANDS FLOATING IN A TENSION WEB; STRESSED LIKE AN AIRPLANE

R. BUCKMINSTER FULLER

120 MILES AN HOUR ON A 90 HP ENGINE

TURNS ON ITS OWN LENGTH

1933–1934

DYMAXION   THREE–WHEELED AUTO

DYMAXION AIROCEAN WORLD 1943

NORTH–SOUTH WORLD

"You do not belong to you. You belong to the universe. The significance of you will forever remain obscure to you, but you may assume that you are fulfilling your significance if you apply yourself to converting all your experience to highest advantage of others. You and all men are here for the sake of other men."   —R. BUCKMINSTER FULLER

OBSERVATIONS & REFLECTIONS

FREE SPIRITS/REBEL VOICES • 10–11

The emerging commercialism of the nineteenth century, with its emphasis on social status and acquisition as a form of identity, was deeply troubling to Henry David Thoreau. He sought to enlarge his horizons beyond moneymaking by searching for the insights offered through his daily contact with nature, insights to which those who were immersed in society were indifferent. For Thoreau, woods, sky, and water enriched human existence far more than anything that could be gained from domesticated, industrialized, urban life. Many Americans today seek a similar relationship with the natural world.

Clarence Darrow's interests, on the other hand, lay elsewhere. After defending Eugene V. Debs in connection with the Pullman strike of 1894, Darrow gave up his lucrative law practice to defend the underdog. His magnificent courtroom skills made him the best-known defense lawyer of his time. Darrow's style was bombastic, provocative, angry, and manipulative. During his career he was once tried for jury tampering. After his acquittal, the prosecutor suggested that Darrow hadn't bribed the jurors, he'd frightened them to death.

Darrow charged no fee for his defense of John T. Scopes—a trial he called "the first case of its kind since we stopped trying people for witchcraft." He lost the case but left the main witness for the prosecution, William Jennings Bryan, exhausted and discredited. Bryan, a self-proclaimed Bible expert, died a few days after the trial.

PILGRIMS AND PURITANS
QUAKERS AND SHAKERS • 12–13

If the *Mayflower* hadn't missed its landfall and landed in New England instead of Virginia, we might be eating Roanoke apple dumplings at Thanksgiving instead of pumpkin pie.

Of the hundred or more passengers aboard the *Mayflower*, only thirty-seven were Pilgrims from Leiden, Holland. With a useless charter for Virginia, the Plymouth Bay Pilgrims formulated the Mayflower Compact as an instrument with which to govern themselves. Ideally suited for the post, William Bradford was elected governor of the colony thirty times in succession.

In our elementary school plays we often cast the Pilgrims and the Puritans in the same roles, but there is a fundamental difference. The Plymouth Bay Pilgrims were self-effacing; they wanted only to be left alone to live and worship in their own way. The Massachusetts Bay Puritans had a mission; they set out to make a godly community for the world to admire and emulate. They wanted to convert others to their way and failing that, impose their way on others. The Massachusetts Bay Colony, larger and more powerful, ultimately absorbed Plymouth.

The Puritans were intolerant and narrow in their beliefs. They saw their lives in terms of duty and obligation rather than pleasure, and they were a powerful influence on the colonial New England mentality—strong, astringent, ethical, energetic, and upright.

❀ ❀ ❀

The religious Society of Friends, commonly called Quakers, regarded the sacraments of the church as nonessential to Christian life. They refused to worship in established churches and refused to pay tithes. They refused to take oaths and were opposed to war. They believed in the equality of all men and women and wouldn't remove their hats before so-called superiors. They were philanthropic. They took the lead in the effort to abolish slavery. They worked for prison reform, the abolishment of capital punishment, and the betterment of common education.

William Penn admired and respected the Native Americans at a time when most colonists showed very little sense of honor in their dealings with them. Penn and the Delaware chief Lapowinsa negotiated the Walking Purchase of 1686 for as much land as a man could cover walking in a day and a half. An honorable agreement between honorable men, it lasted for fifty years. After Penn's death unscrupulous land speculators renegotiated a treaty in which instead of one man walking, three men ran. They could thereby cover some sixty miles, and the Delaware lost most of their land.

❀ ❀ ❀

There is no known portrait of Mother Ann Lee. The Shaker woman depicted is meant to suggest the indomitable spirit of the founder of the Shaker community in this country, the first communistic society in America.

The Shakers, an offshoot of the Quakers, sought to worship God after their peculiar manner of marching or dancing, singing and shaking. According to William K. Sanford of Colonie, New York, "The Shakers were two hundred years ahead of time in their belief in and insistence on applying the concepts of human rights to all human relationships, a concept which is reflected in today's court decisions, legislative enactments, and public attitude."

MAVERICK MINISTERS/GUIDING LIGHTS • 14–15

Legend has it that Colonel Samuel A. Maverick, a Texas attorney, neglected to brand a herd of one hundred longhorns he had received as a fee for services. An interested buyer, Toutant Beauregard, was quick to discover the longhorns were unbranded. He marked them with his own brand and claimed them for himself. The term *maverick* is now used for a yearling or a calf that strays from its mother. It has another contemporary usage—a dissenter who takes an independent stand apart from his associates.

❀ ❀ ❀

Roger Williams, a Puritan preacher, was banished from the Massachusetts Bay Colony (1635) because he believed that all people should have the freedom to choose their own form of worship. Williams, the founder of Rhode Island, pursued the ideals of democracy and humanitarianism. His colony became a refuge from religious persecution.

By the beginning of the eighteenth century, the concept of religious freedom was making inroads even in the strict Bible communities of New England. Puritanical "hellfire and damnation" sermons were losing their effectiveness until our earliest revival movement, the Great Awakening. The fervent preaching of Jonathan Edwards, the foremost theologian of the time, brought many New Englanders back to the fold. However, rationalism and secularism were firmly established by the time the Constitution of the United States was written (1787). The First Amendment to it was added as a further guarantee of religious freedom (1791).

In the nineteenth century, the Industrial Revolution made further inroads on religious institutions, replacing them with secular substitutes—patriotism and capitalism.

By now our holy days are holidays. But historians Will and Ariel Durant point out that "one lesson of history is that religion has many lives, and a habit of resurrection." The enthusiastic ranks of back-to-the-Bible fundamentalists, the emergence of the Church of Jesus Christ of Latter-Day Saints as a magnet for young people, and the mosques and minarets dotting the Midwest suggest they are right.

❀ ❀ ❀

The first Bible printed in the colonies was John Eliot's translation into the Algonquian language. The Bible's longest word is *Wutappesittukqussunnookwehtunkquoh*—"kneeling down to him."

❀ ❀ ❀

The first public elementary school offering free education for all opened its doors in 1812, and from that day onward dedicated educators set about improving our school system. Horace Mann, often called the Father of Public Schools, was one of our most effective administrators. He improved academic standards and was an early advocate of coeducation.

William H. McGuffey helped organize the common-school system of Ohio but is chiefly remembered as the compiler of the Eclectic Readers series. The influence of these "readers" in shaping the minds of mid-nineteenth-century Americans can hardly be exaggerated. Although they never took hold in New England, 122 million copies of McGuffey's books were sold nationwide. All of them portrayed America as a land of opportunity, and all had one moral lesson: diligence brings success and success is synonymous with wealth.

Oddly enough, while he was certainly diligent, McGuffey didn't get rich. He *did* make millionaires of ten publishers. A story has it that each year at Christmas one of his publishers would send him a barrel of hams.

❀ ❀ ❀

Horatio Alger, Jr.—whose more than one hundred books for boys were described as being "good and wholesome with enough 'ginger' in them to suit the tastes of the younger generation"—elaborated on McGuffey's theme: pluck and luck, industry and frugality brought you from rags to riches. Judging from some of Alger's titles, if you were *Brave and Bold*, *Slow and Sure*, *Strong and Steady*, and could *Do and Dare*, you were *Bound to Rise*. Education didn't seem to have a role to play in this do-it-yourself success story.

Certainly the philosopher John Dewey didn't believe a word of this. In the beginning of the twentieth century his interest was in another kind of success. He believed that schools should be responsible for saturating the student "with the spirit of service, and providing him with the instruments of effective self-direction," thereby giving us the "best guarantee of a larger society which is worthy, lovely, and harmonious."

At the end of the twentieth century, the bad news, according to writer Tracy Kidder, is that "many tests and surveys show that large percentages of American youth come out of high school and even college incompetent in the three R's and ignorant of basic facts about history, geography, science, and literature." The good news is that "the history of education in the twentieth century presents a picture of a nation perennially dissatisfied...with its public schools" and again, "the history of education in America is the history of attempts to reform it."

THE IMPASSIONED FIGHTS FOR
FREEDOM AND EQUAL RIGHTS • 16–17

Almost all of the early participants in the fight for the abolition of slavery were nonviolent. Some were militant with words, writing and lecturing or lobbying for freedom. Others took more direct action by helping enslaved blacks to escape—hiding them, transporting them, relocating them in the North.

John Brown was an anti-slavery activist who was not satisfied with peaceful protests against slavery. Asserting that he was an instrument in the hand of God, he rationalized his violence as necessary to furthering the cause of emancipation. In the role of fighter for freedom he became a northern hero and a cause célèbre. He believed that a *little* violence would go a long way. With twenty-one armed followers, he seized the federal arsenal at Harpers Ferry, West Virginia, intent on converting it into a fortress in which everyone desiring to be free might find sanctuary. His unsuccessful foray led to his indictment on charges of "treason, servile insurrection, and murder." He was tried, found guilty, and sentenced to hang. On his way to the gallows, he handed a note to one of his guards. It read: "I, John Brown, am now quite *certain* that the crimes of this *guilty land; will* never be purged *away;* but with Blood. I had *as I now think:* vainly flattered myself that without *very much* bloodshed it might be done."

He was right, of course. It took the Civil War, the bloodiest conflict in our country's history, to end slavery.

❀ ❀ ❀

The fight for woman suffrage followed the same pattern as the fight to end slavery—from peaceful dialogue to violent action. The first women's rights conference took place in Seneca Falls, New York, in 1848. There a Declaration of Sentiments was drafted that included a resolution that women should fight for the vote. Most Americans felt that respectable women should not publicly demonstrate to make their demands known. Newspaper editors and preachers—indeed, the nation at large—met the declaration with derision and ridicule.

Susan B. Anthony and Elizabeth Cady Stanton led the woman suffrage movement for more than sixty years. Petitions, pamphlets, parades, conventions, women's organizations, publications, and agitation produced rather meager results, other than a gradual transformation of public opinion as to the rights of women.

It was up to the next generation of activists, in the early 1900s, to take up the cause. Using the methods of the British leader Emmeline Pankhurst and her suffragettes, Alice Paul led American women in a new strategy of militant defiance. Women picketing the White House enraged unruly crowds of men. Far from protecting the women, the police were soon leading the attacks and arresting them. In jail, enduring increasingly stiff sentences, they were subjected to beatings and forced feeding when they used hunger strikes as a form of protest, and they were allowed no visitors and no legal counsel for extended periods.

The White House was flooded with angry letters. President Woodrow Wilson finally agreed to the release of all jailed suffragists and helped to push the Woman Suffrage Amendment (Article XIX) through Congress in 1920.

The Fifteenth Amendment, following on the heels of the end of slavery, gave black men the right to vote in 1870. It took another fifty years for American women to be guaranteed the same right.

WARRIORS AND PATRIOTS • 18–19

The Gatling gun, the first practical machine gun, was patented in 1862 by Dr. Richard J. Gatling of North Carolina. Dr. Gatling seriously believed that the deadliness of his weapon would discourage the human race from fighting. The *gat,* a world traveler, has been responsible for the deaths of more than eight million human beings.

At about the same time, the Nobel works in Heleneborg, Sweden, manufactured mines, torpedoes, and high explosives. Alfred Bernhard Nobel, the inventor of dynamite, uneasy about his family's and his own role in the development of such potentially dangerous weapons, created a fund to award annual prizes to the persons who had done the most to promote international peace. Since 1901, when the first Nobel Peace Prize was awarded, fifteen Americans have received it.

❀ ❀ ❀

Speaking to General James Longstreet at the battle of Fredericksburg, Virginia, General Robert E. Lee said, "It is well that war is so terrible—we would grow too fond of it." But fond of it we are. In the last 3,448 years of recorded history, only 268 years have been without a war in some part of the world.

War seems to be the method by which issues of expansion, competition, national pride, and diplomacy are decided. With universal conscription and the existence of nonselective bombs, no one of any age or either sex is exempt from involvement, and in the late twentieth century, with the naïveté of those earlier inventor pacifists, some Americans now think of war as having a humanitarian role: war cannot only end *war* but end starvation and ignorance as well.

❀ ❀ ❀

Margaret (called Molly) Corbin fought with Proctor's Artillery at Fort Washington, New York. Molly Hays, who began her military career as a water girl, was nicknamed Molly Pitcher. She fought at Monmouth, New Jersey, as a cannoneer. The two Mollys were in two of the hottest actions of the Revolution, under the aegis of a woman, Saint Barbara, the patron saint of the artillery. Women have been involved in every military action since the founding of our country. Even in the thirty days of the Persian Gulf War, fifteen servicewomen died.

❀ ❀ ❀

Seven of our fighting generals have been rewarded with terms as president of the United States: George Washington, Andrew Jackson, William Henry Harrison, Zachary Taylor, Ulysses S. Grant, James Garfield, and Dwight D. Eisenhower.

❀ ❀ ❀

There are many monuments to the unknown soldiers of this country but few to the truly unknown—the thousands of black soldiers who fought for the Union Army during the Civil War.

PICTORIAL HISTORIANS
THE FOURTH ESTATE • 20–21

Daguerreotype, a French invention, was the earliest photographic process. Used in America between 1839 and the 1850s, it produced one-of-a-kind images on a silver-coated plate. Its shiny, reflective surfaces caused Dr. Oliver Wendell Holmes to call the process "the mirror with a memory." Daguerreotypes were an instant success, and daguerrean portrait studios sprang up everywhere.

The collodion wet-plate negative, developed in 1851 and used until 1881, was the first practical method for making a photographic image on glass. The glass negative could be used to make multiple photographic prints. Mathew Brady, the best-known photographer of the Civil War, used this process. A fashionable portraitist, he set off from Washington, D.C., for the Bull Run battlefield in northern Virginia because, he said, "a spirit in my feet said 'go' and I went."

Taking pictures in the field using the wet-plate method was a daunting affair. The heavy photographic equipment had to be carried on an accompanying wagon. The photographer removed an eight-by-ten-inch glass plate from its dust-proof box, sensitized it in the total darkness of the wagon, hurried to the camera, tripped the shutter, then rushed the plate back to the wagon for developing.

This complex process was also used by Eadweard Muybridge for his studies of animal locomotion. He had a horse gallop along a measured path in front of a bank of cameras, each with a fine thread attached to the shutter. As the horse galloped, it broke the threads, triggering an instantaneous picture. His zoopraxiscope, which projected sequential pictures on a screen (1881), is considered to be a forerunner of the motion picture.

❀ ❀ ❀

George Eastman developed and perfected the dry-plate process and invented transparent film. He named his company and his cameras *Kodak* because the word had no meaning in any language. His hand-held Kodak Brownie, which sold for a dollar in 1901, made photographers of us all.

❀ ❀ ❀

Autochromes, produced by a now-obsolete method of color photography, were exhibited by Alfred Stieglitz in 1907. It wasn't until the mid-twentieth century that color photographs came into common use in magazines—*LIFE* in particular—and for portraiture and snapshots.

❀ ❀ ❀

The term *estate* was originally used to designate organized classes of society with separate voices in government. The three classes were: the nobility, the clergy, and the commons (knights and townspeople of substance). *The Fourth Estate,* a term often used today, refers to a group (outside the usual powers) that influences the country's politics; the term also denotes the members of the press.

❀ ❀ ❀

The New York *Tribune* was published for 125 years—43,483 daily issues. Its founder, Horace Greeley, guaranteed a newspaper "worthy of the virtuous and refined, and a welcome visitant at the family fireside." Greeley advocated tax-supported public schools, organization of labor, profit sharing, and employer/employee ownership. He opposed monopolies, including grants to railroads. Greeley was against slavery and demanded that President Lincoln commit himself to emancipation.

President Abraham Lincoln commented to an aide, "No man, whether he be private citizen or President of the United States, can successfully carry on a controversy with a great newspaper and escape destruction unless he owns a newspaper equally great with a circulation in the same neighborhood."

❀ ❀ ❀

Greeley's *The New Yorker* was discontinued; it has no connection to the magazine of the same name that is published today.

THE MAGNETIC WEST: PATHFINDERS,
SETTLERS, AND IMAGE MAKERS • 22–23

The story of the settling of the American West is our national drama, our fairy tale, our morality play, our epic saga. Its cast of characters includes: The Explorers, The Noble Savages, The Intrepid Pioneers, and those archetypal folk heroes, The Cowboys. Its scenery: The Plains, The Mountains. Its props: The Six-shooter, The Conestoga Wagon. Its extras: The Hunters, The Trappers, The Guides, The U.S. Cavalry, The Cow Pony, and The Buffalo.

But the true West, which was even more remarkable than its myths, represented many different things to different people. It was a frightening wilderness. It was a new land to explore, to conquer, and to settle. It was a vast forest, a mighty mountain range. It was free land. It was a new start in life—a second chance. It was an agrarian bonanza as well as a gold mine. It was hardship and isolation. It was adventure. It helped to shape the American consciousness, and created our native costume—boot-cut blue jeans.

RADICAL REFORMERS AND
HUMANITARIANS • 24–25

Henry Bergh was the president, inspirer, advocate, lecturer, writer, administrator, fund-raiser, and founder of the American Society for the Prevention of Cruelty to Animals (ASPCA), the first organization in the Western Hemisphere to protest the abuse of animals. In the nineteenth century, there was much to protest.

Gentlemen sportsmen at "pigeon shoots" blinded birds to create more interesting flight patterns; the not-so-gentlemanly flocked to fighting pits to watch and gamble on exhibitions of terriers fighting rats, bulldogs fighting black bears, and cocks fighting each other. At city pounds, dogs were executed with unspeakable cruelty; live calves were transported tied together like cordwood; butchers plucked living poultry; and overworked dray horses stumbled before overloaded wagons. These barbarous acts were made illegal under the Animal-Welfare Act (1866). Bergh devoted his life to seeing that the law was enforced.

Before he was through, he had given kindness a new dimension. His legacy is a network of anti-cruelty societies, animal rescue leagues, and placement services for stray and abandoned animals. But Bergh didn't stop there. He and his associate Elbridge T. Gerry established the New York Society for the Prevention of Cruelty to Children (1874).

⚘ ⚘ ⚘

The Gilded Age, the Gay Nineties, the "Good Old Days"—terms applied to the period between the Civil War and the early 1900s—found humanity at risk as well as animals. The "good old days" were good for the privileged few, but for the mass of Americans the period was one of unrelenting hardship.

It is hard to imagine the conditions under which people lived in the urban slums of the Gilded Age: the overcrowded tenements, the uncollected garbage, the lack of sanitation, the open sewers, the unlighted streets, the untreated disease, and the long work hours, the sweatshops, the child labor, the industrial machinery without safeguards, the cruelty of men to women, parents to children—and the multitude of half-starved, unwanted children.

We owe a great debt to reformers Jane Addams, Jacob Riis, Margaret Sanger, and others like them for creating a profound change in the moral climate of America.

MEGA-MILLIONAIRES: INDUSTRIALISTS, FINANCIERS, AND ROBBER BARONS • 26–27

The early self-made millionaires of America created colossal financial and industrial empires. They also created an aristocracy of wealth. Gratifying their social ambitions, they indulged in yachts and huge villas, Fifth Avenue and Nob Hill mansions, collections of Old Masters and libraries of first editions. Their sons and daughters married within their group or sought titled Europeans. The crowning symbol of economic and social achievement, in a class by itself, was the private railway car—often fitted with crystal chandeliers, wine "cellars," Tiffany tableware, and gold plumbing fixtures (said to be economical in the long run because they needed no polishing).

By 1900 these First Families were the Lords of Creation, the Princes of Industry, the Grand Acquisitors, and there were only a handful of them. They monopolized the country's resources, paid the wages of millions of workers, and as buyers, shippers, and processors of timber, livestock, and agricultural products, affected the lives of most other American families. Their monopolies, trusts, syndicates, and interlocking corporations were subject to no government regulatory agencies; there were no income taxes. They answered only to their own consciences, which told them that they deserved their millions.

Peter Cooper was an exception. Derisively called "the self-made millionaire glue-boiler," he invested his glue profits in Manhattan real estate. The value of his real estate soared. He reinvested in and expanded his own company, and Providence smiled on him, rewarding his virtuous traits.

Cooper was thrifty, sober, industrious, and self-reliant. He kept no formal books, thought of banks and bankers as creations of Satan, never borrowed a cent, and paid his obligations in gold. Making money, to him, was irrelevant—it was simply a reward for moral behavior and for providing the world with a few useful products: glue, neat's-foot oil, isinglass, gelatin, and his railway engine named Tom Thumb.

Peter Cooper was America's first munificent philanthropist. His example started dozens of other millionaires on this unlikely path.

⚘ ⚘ ⚘

In John Bunyan's The Pilgrim's Progress, there is a tale about a Man with a Muckrake who, when offered a crown, keeps his head down and continues to rake the filth off the floor. Teddy Roosevelt said that this story reminded him of certain writers of political exposés, and muckraker be-

came a cherished title of honor. Ida Tarbell, a historical researcher for McClure's Magazine, was one of the first to earn it. Asked to write a series of articles about the Standard Oil Company, she worked several years to produce a literary indictment of Standard Oil—a story of corruption, privilege, and crushed competition. Tarbell's articles inspired muckraking exposés in other magazines: articles about stock manipulations, meatpacking scandals, unscrupulous financial speculations, fake medical products, and corrupt U.S. senators.

⚘ ⚘ ⚘

A bucolic retreat for Pittsburgh industrialists whose factories had already begun to pollute the air and water around them, the South Fork Fishing and Hunting Club was said to have caused the Johnstown Flood. The club's man-made lake was seventy feet deep and contained twenty million tons of water. Its poorly engineered earthen dam, which served no purpose but to provide sports facilities for the pleasure of a few rich men, burst on May 31, 1889, flooding the narrow valley of the South Fork Creek. More than two thousand people were left dead in its wake. The club's official contribution to the relief effort was a thousand used blankets.

THE WOBBLIES AND THE MINERS: SHOCK TROOPS OF THE AFL-CIO • 28–29

In 1876 the western hard-rock miners were paid three dollars a day for eight to twelve hours of brutal labor. Working underground, in constant danger of accidents and the deadly lung diseases peculiar to the industry, the miners saw unionism as their only hope for bettering their wages and working conditions. Their early union, the Western Federation of Miners, challenged the mine owners in some of the most violent confrontations in the annals of the West. After twenty-five years of struggle, the miners saw the death of their union. They were still making only three dollars a day.

The Western Federation was a failure, but it laid the groundwork for, and was the nucleus of, a new union, the short-lived, revolutionary Industrial Workers of the World, nicknamed the Wobblies. Founded in 1905, the IWW's aim was to unite all workers, skilled and unskilled, in industrywide unions. Although the Wobblies made several contributions to the labor movement, particularly among migrant workers and lumberjacks, their direct and often violent action—and their anti-militarist stand during World War I—caused their leader, William "Big Bill" Haywood, to be tried for sedition. Lesser leaders were jailed for draft evasion and sabotage. Without them the membership of the IWW declined. Except for their songs, the Wobblies are scarcely remembered.

One of the founders of the IWW, Eugene V. Debs, was a giant among labor leaders and radical politicians. He was a brilliant and impassioned orator. Debs in 1893 organized the industrywide American Railway Union. He was jailed for defying a court injunction during the Pullman strike of 1894. In jail, through his reading, Debs discovered Socialism. Ultimately his socialist ideals caused him to break with the Wobblies. The Socialists and the Wobblies shared many of the same goals, but they differed on how to achieve them. Debs believed in the ballot box. He ran for president five times on the Socialist Party ticket, the last time while he was serving a ten-year sentence in jail for speaking out as a pacifist against World War I and the wartime Espionage Acts of 1917 and 1918. In the 1920 presidential election he got 915,000 votes.

⚘ ⚘ ⚘

The United Mine Workers of America, the first major industrywide union, included miners, sorters, electricians, motormen, and many unskilled eleven-year-old boys. Led first by John Mitchell, from 1898–1908, and later, for forty years, by John L. Lewis, the miners, by 1949, were the best-paid industrial workers. Following the miners' example, the shipbuilding, steel, oil, transportation, automobile, and newspaper industries organized. They affiliated themselves with Lewis's newly formed Congress of Industrial Organizations (CIO). When the CIO merged with the craft unions' American Federation of Labor (AFL) in 1955, the resultant AFL-CIO became an immensely powerful force in American politics and economics.

THE PASTORAL PROTECTORS: NATURALISTS AND ECOLOGISTS • 30–31

John Burroughs was once the most popular nature writer in the United States. In flowery prose he described rural life and the pre-industrial world as idyllic, but his incongruous friendships with industrialists—Harvey Firestone, Thomas Edison, and Henry Ford, who made their livings exploiting the natural world—tarnished his posthumous reputation.

When Burroughs wrote an essay characterizing cars as despoilers of nature, Ford gave him a Model T, and Burroughs was soon photographed touring the country. Still, he left us with an appealing rose-tinted vision of simple rural living.

John Muir, more politically active and possibly more sophisticated than Burroughs, was a tireless conservationist. Along with Theodore Roosevelt he sought to halt the exhaustion of timberlands by private industry. Muir Woods National Monument, a virgin stand of redwoods in California, is named after him.

⚘ ⚘ ⚘

We live in an age when an unblemished, shiny waxed skin on an apple is more important to us than its nutritional content. We pay a great price for such aesthetically pleasing crops.

Rachel Carson was one of the first to explore the idea that ecology relates to daily living, "that the central problem of our age has...become the contamination of man's total environment," and that the balance of nature must not be tampered with. When a neighbor wrote to her of the death of fourteen robins after the pesticide DDT had been sprayed in her yard, Carson embarked on a whole new project for her life's work—to teach us of the dangers of the chemicals we had assumed were safe to use.

Grace Paley points out that Carson "taught us that the life of a bug cannot be taken without silencing songbirds. And finally the songbird cannot be silenced without poisoning the human child."

⚘ ⚘ ⚘

Euthenics: the science concerned with bettering the condition of human beings through the improvement of their environment. The term was coined by Ellen Swallow Richards.

WORKER IN THE VINEYARD ECCENTRIC AUTOCRAT • 32–33

In the late 1960s Cesar Chavez organized one hundred thousand migrant workers into the first viable farmworkers union in the United States. Using La Causa (a labor and civil rights organization with religious overtones) as a rallying point and ¡Viva La Huelga! ("Strike!") as a rallying cry, and religious fasts and boycotts of lettuce and table grapes as tactics, he and the United Farm Workers took on the unionization of the $4 billion California agribusiness, with mixed results.

"We have lost perhaps the greatest Californian of the twentieth century," the president of the California State Senate said of him, when Chavez was safely in his grave. An estimated thirty-five thousand people marched in Chavez's funeral cortege.

⚘ ⚘ ⚘

Henry Ford didn't invent the moving assembly-line production technique, but he did develop it to remarkable perfection. Thanks to Ford, the automobile, formerly a plaything for the rich, became within reach of the average American family. The construction of his reasonably priced Model T was so simple that many minor repairs could be made with hairpins, baling wire, and chewing gum. Americans were overjoyed by an unprecedented mobility and took to the roads in an enthusiastic rediscovery of America.

In 1909 the United States had 725 miles of paved rural roads. By 1930 there was a network of one hundred thousand miles, crisscrossing the country, turning an inaccessible wilderness into a connected community of filling stations, parking lots, trucking services, bus lines, roadside advertising, tourist cabins, diners, suburbs, and factories, and encouraging a growing need for installment buying and used cars.

Saluting the "flivver," which was responsible for most of the traffic jams of the twenties, humorist Will Rogers declared, "So good luck,

Mr. Ford. It will take a hundred years to tell whether you have helped us or hurt us, but you certainly didn't leave us the way you found us."

The hundred years is almost up.

EXPATRIATES: AMERICANS ABROAD • 34–35

Americans have a long tradition of travel and study abroad. Almost all of our best-known writers have spent a year or two on the Continent. American painters and sculptors have filled Parisian studios and roamed Italian ruins. Benjamin Franklin, Benjamin West, and Washington Irving lived for extended periods in England and France.

Still, until the end of the last century it was almost unheard of for Americans to take up permanent residence abroad. Those who did—and those who do—did so for a variety of reasons. Henry James found that America lacked many amenities. We had "no sovereign, no court, no personal loyalty, no aristocracy, no church…no army…no country gentlemen, no palaces, no castles, nor manors, nor old country-houses, nor parsonages, nor thatched cottages, nor ivied ruins; no cathedrals, nor abbeys, nor little Norman churches; no great Universities nor public schools…no literature, no novels, no museums, no pictures, no political society, no sporting class…The elements of high civilization, as it exists in other countries…are absent."

❂ ❂ ❂

Other expatriates railed against American puritanism, American crudeness, American racism, and the restrictions of life in small-town America. They sought a more satisfying intellectual life than they found at home, or some relief from racial discrimination. However, many of the self-exiled found that a geographical change didn't necessarily provide a magical reprieve from their dissatisfactions and returned home. Even Henry James discovered, "There comes a time when one set of customs, wherever it may be found, grows to seem to you about as provincial as another."

❂ ❂ ❂

Gertrude Stein, best known for "Rose is a rose is a rose," called the Americans living in Paris in the '20s "a lost generation."

WRITERS: FICTION, HISTORY, ESSAYS, PLAYS, AND CRITICISM • 36–37

The authors included on these pages represent one of the splendors of American culture—its literature—and the contribution it has made to the world's letters.

America's writers come from every walk of life: the leisure class, the working class, the educated elite, and even the high school dropouts. Their work is original, audacious, a mixture of beauty and strangeness.

❂ ❂ ❂

There is a good reason why most reflections on American literature include a paragraph about *Moby Dick*. Contemporary novelist Rikki Ducornet, for example, writes: "Herman Melville (neglected in his lifetime) wrote a book about the horrors of obsessive hatred and abusive authority, but also about the essential search for wholeness and for knowledge. *Moby Dick*, flamboyantly imagined, encyclopedic in its conception, rooted in philosophical speculation, illumined by psychological insight, is the archetypal American novel. Its influence is worldwide."

❂ ❂ ❂

The authors of books for young people depicted here are included not because their books have exceptional literary merit but because they represent a popular genre. These authors wrote some of the most widely read books ever published in America. The boyish "morality plays" of Horatio Alger, L. Frank Baum's fantasies of Oz, Louisa May Alcott's high-spirited *Little Women*, and the key to our English literary heritage that Frances Hodgson Burnett provided when she opened the gate to *The Secret Garden*—all were part of a youthful America's literary coming of age.

POETS/POETS OF MOTION • 38–39

Walt Whitman, arguably America's greatest poet, was very much a part of the world. He edited a newspaper, worked as a carpenter, taught in country schools, and was active in Democratic Party politics. He fraternized with fishermen and farmers. He was a reformer who zealously plunged into humanitarian movements. However, his *real* occupation was to mingle with crowds while he simultaneously tried his hand at a new kind of verse.

Whitman abandoned the stock poetic plots of heroes, love, war, and high personages. No legend, no myth, no euphemism finds its way into his work. His style is one of great originality, homely and idiomatic; bereft of rhyme and meter, it follows the rhythms of nature.

Whitman believed that nations should act for the good of mankind. He believed that America was one of the greatest of nations—not a conqueror but healthy and free, and peaceable. He allowed his poetry to express the vitality of Americans—their physicality, their pride, their compassion, and their sympathy for people struggling for freedom.

He printed and published his own work.

❂ ❂ ❂

Emily Dickinson was a recluse, totally withdrawn from the world. She had an energy of spirit and mind that only the rarest of poets possess. Her vocabulary is inventive; her imagery is unpredictable. She invests familiar objects with magic; her natural world is microscopic and filled with mysteries and grandeur.

She wrote her poems on scraps of notepaper, sewed them together, tied them up in bundles with string or ribbon, and tucked them away in her desk or bureau drawers. When she died she left word to have her poems burned, but her sister, Lavinia, saved them. Dickinson's poems began to appear in print four years after her death.

Emily Dickinson and Walt Whitman were visionaries and acute individualists. Their poems illustrate the paradox contained not only in American letters but in all art: that a private world, introspective and seemingly unique, may produce a work so authentic, so human that it informs an entire culture. American poetry knows no geographic boundaries but holds up a mirror of possibility, offering us a glimpse of the deeply felt and imagined life we can all aspire to.

❂ ❂ ❂

Dancing is the oldest art; it existed before music; it can be independent of it. Its components are space, time, and human bodies. The language of dance needs no words; it communicates through symbols, beyond ordinary speech. But because dance forms reflect human habits and activities, they adapt and change as humans change.

Folk dancing, ballroom dancing, classical ballet—indeed, all the genres of dance have been renewed and refreshed by the innovations of the fine American dancer-choreographers of the twentieth century. Breaking taboos, tapping grassroots, jumping for joy, their dances have clarity, humor, athleticism, and exciting new formats that delight dancers and spectators alike.

AMERICAN ARCHITECTS: THE SHAPES OF DEMOCRACY • 40–41

Architecture is intimately connected to the comforts of life. In seeking those comforts, we Americans have always built our shelters much the way we have wanted to, needed to, or could. The first Americans used the building materials at hand: branches, thatch, adobe, skins, sod, or ice. Given more time, more land, more resources, and more skills, later settlers treated themselves to log houses, rough-sawed saltboxes, and handsome colonial frame houses in New England and pillared plantation homes in the South.

Our public architecture owes much of its character to the influence of President Thomas Jefferson. A true lover of antiquity who had a special affection for all that was Roman and noble, Jefferson paid particular attention to the planning of Washington, D.C., and the building of the University of Virginia. Moving west, migrating Americans carried their Bibles and "builders handbooks" with them, dotting the Ohio Valley and the middle states with miniature Greek and Roman temples.

As the nation prospered, Americans built Renaissance railway stations and museums, Baroque cottages with carpenter Gothic ornamentation, Italian villas, French châteaux, and Romanesque warehouses and factories.

While McKim, Mead, and White and their followers were obliging their wealthy patrons in the East with spurious palaces, Chicago millionaires were tending to nothing but business, and Chicago architects were making business buildings for businessmen. Ornamentation was modified in favor of expanded space and simplicity. Louis Sullivan, who deplored the eclecticism and unalloyed fakery of the eastern architects, became the unchallenged master of the skyscraper. But he was an idealist.

The rest of us—given steel, reinforced concrete, and electricity—can still indulge in even greater heights of imagination and flights of fancy. There are no limitations on the opulence and glitter of our sky-high buildings, our luxury hotels, our family theme parks, our glass houses—and the lights of Las Vegas.

THE VISUAL ARTISTS • 42–43

Benjamin West was the first of our great artist-teachers. His school in London continued the traditional link between Colonial and Revolutionary artists and the English style of painting. One of the best of his pupils, Gilbert Stuart, became the foremost artist of the Federal period. Two of West's most famous students turned to other forms of creative effort because they didn't believe their art was properly appreciated. Samuel F. B. Morse developed the telegraph. Robert Fulton built a steamboat and put it into common use.

Gradually, as our painters found their art relating more to their lives in America than to the artistic traditions inherited from Europe, a movement sometimes referred to as an American Renaissance began. Today it is difficult to imagine a museum anywhere in the world that does not include paintings *of America by* Americans in an American style, with all its variety and creativity. From epic landscapes to persuasive portraits, from urban realism to abstract expressionism and pop art, our quintessentially homegrown painting and sculpture changed our image of ourselves and influenced the world's view of us.

ENDURING ICONS: ENTERTAINERS, IMPRESARIOS, AND SUPERSTARS • 44–45

Americans have an insatiable appetite for entertainment in all its forms, and as quickly as those forms change, they are wholeheartedly embraced. The most recent form of entertainment is the computer. In addition to being a magical business machine, it connects people to an international network of fun and competitive games.

Logging on to a computer may someday replace going to the library, the theater, the concert hall, and the dinner party, but it is hard to believe it will ever replace going to the movies. How can it? The movies and their stepchildren, television and videos, have become our history books, our geographies, our novels, our comedies and tragedies, our baby-sitters, and our cures for insomnia. Movie stars are our royalty. They provide us with our fantasies, our beauty hints, our role models, our nostalgia, and our scandals.

Thomas Edison couldn't possibly have imagined how his little nickel machine would enchant the human race—or that his rolls of film would encircle the globe.

COMPOSERS, CLASSY TUNESMITHS, AND ALL THAT JAZZ • 46–47

In the nineteenth century American composers and musicians took their cues from Old World modes. Scottish and Irish lilts influenced our folk songs; African music formed the basis of gospel singing; American classical musicians continued to develop European forms. Music was handed to us on a plate. But all truly *American* music begins with jazz.

Emerging from the mean streets of urban ghettos, jazz is the music of an oppressed people. In the words of pianist, composer, and orchestrator Luther Henderson, "Jazz is a matter of personal and one-to-one release. It's a matter of getting it out. If you go into the basic background of any ethnic group, you will find the people on the bottom making musical expressions that have not only to do with release, but with the eternal hope that they will be released. I suspect the harder the foot gets put on the neck, the more poignant is the expression of pain and hope that comes out."

Jazz is different from all other music by virtue of its melody, harmony, rhythm, and improvisational nature; it is indigenous to our country; it is a unique art form. From classical composition to musical comedy, from ragtime to rap, jazz is the major influence on contemporary American music.

THE GREAT NATIONAL PASTIME: PACESETTERS AND GROUNDBREAKERS • 48–49

Americans have played baseball in one form or another, in one place or another, for more than two hundred years. We play it in backyards and prison yards, in city alleys and vacant lots, in farmers' pastures, on playgrounds, and on playing fields.

Baseball is played by amateurs and professionals, by men, women, and children. It is a slow game demanding lightning speed. Its greatest heroes are players who fail to hit the ball seven times out of ten. Ken Burns and Geoffrey C. Ward called it a mythic game—"a haunted game in which every player is measured against the ghosts of all who have gone before."

Baseball has turned news reporters into poets and columnists into national treasures. Sportswriters competed to coin nicknames that would do justice to the power of Babe Ruth. The doggerel of Franklin P. Adams immortalized the "trio of bear cubs," Tinker and Evers and Chance. Grantland Rice, Damon Runyon, John Kieran, Heywood Broun, Paul Gallico, and Ring Lardner were robust writers of the first half of the twentieth century who included sports in their repertoires and did much to foster interest in baseball as a spectator sport. The pioneer black sportswriters Wendell Smith and Mabray Kountze chronicled the victories of talented black players over prejudice and segregation.

Radio and television, in their turn, made sporting events accessible to millions of Americans who had paid no prior attention to the games. Not only baseball but football, basketball, hockey, and the Olympic Games were to become mass spectator sports with great commercial importance.

✳ ✳ ✳

Black teams and white teams and their respective leagues coexisted in America for more than ninety years. Baseball Commissioner Kenesaw Mountain Landis, who opposed integration, was partly responsible for this continuing segregation. Happy Chandler, who became commissioner after Landis's death in 1944, turned the tide. When fifteen clubs (out of sixteen) voted to oppose integration, Chandler responded, "If a black can fight for his country in Okinawa and Guadalcanal, he can play organized baseball," thereby settling the issue. Ford Frick, then-president of the National League, backed him up. To rumors that teams would refuse to play the Dodgers if they insisted on hiring a black man, Frick said, "I don't care if half the league strikes. . . . This is the United States of America and one citizen has as much right to play as another."

✳ ✳ ✳

The term *the National Pastime* is credited to the New York *Mercury*, 1856.

SCOUNDRELS AND THIEVES VILLAINS AND ROGUES • 50–51

Portrayed here are not necessarily our hard-core criminals but rather our legendary scoundrels and rogue heroes. They are celebrated for their "derring-do," not for their thefts and murders and income tax frauds. Sometimes they are envied for their adventurous lives outside our laws.

Occasionally our legislation creates a criminal class. There was never a law more flagrantly violated than the unfortunate National Prohibition Act of 1920. Congressman Fiorello H. La Guardia declared it would take a police force of 250,000 to enforce Prohibition in New York City, and added that another 200,000 would be required to police the police.

Often we elect rascals to office to avenge ourselves for perceived economic deprivations or insults to our social status, and then later we complain about the politicians' dishonesty. For some of us such anti-heroes are our alter egos whose actions reveal our greed, our illegal desires, and our suppressed bigotry. We perpetuate their memories in movies and in folk songs. Fortunately, they are far outnumbered by the heroes we genuinely love, admire, and seek to emulate.

INVENTING THE FUTURE: THE INDIVIDUAL GENIUS • 52–53

No particular background explains the individual genius—geniuses emerge at any place and at any time. We were lucky to have one as a framer of the Constitution of the United States, a giant of human history, Benjamin Franklin.

At age twenty-seven Franklin was a writer, the most successful and amusing of his day. He set up his own printing press, ran his own newspaper, and then retired at the age of forty—a retirement that meant plunging himself into another absorbing activity: science, or natural philosophy, as it was known in the eighteenth century.

Long before Franklin flew his famous kite, he had become a world-renowned scientist. The experiments he performed or envisioned were original and crucial; his procedures were analytical and objective. Many terms we still use today originated with Franklin: *charge*, *discharge*, *battery*, *electric shock*, *condenser*, and *electrician*, among others.

✳ ✳ ✳

Thomas Edison was born into a nonconformist family. He was educated by his mother at home; when he did attend school for a few months, he was thought to be feebleminded because he refused to recite in class. He had a chemistry shop in his basement and labeled all the bottles "poison." Edison became a telegrapher and was one of the fastest receivers and transmitters of his time. His earliest inventions were mechanical contraptions that made him appear to be awake when he was actually asleep on the job.

When Edison set up his laboratory in Menlo Park, New Jersey, his business, a kind of Inventions to Order, was essentially a one-man operation, though at times he employed up to one hundred men. But the time when an individual, eccentric inventor could set up his own shop, hold his own patents, and reap the profits from the manufacture of his own devices soon came to a close.

✳ ✳ ✳

In the twentieth century, as science and technology increased in specialization, pioneering laboratories have become the property of large companies and institutions that can better provide the financial resources for scientific breakthroughs. Scientists now work as teams, and prizes are most often shared. Teamwork is so much the order of the day that group thinking has become an area of study for psychologists. But some brilliant individualists continued to succeed outside this new establishment.

Twice recipient of the Nobel Prize, once for chemistry and again for peace, Linus C. Pauling left off picketing the White House in a protest against the testing of nuclear weapons in order to join the White House gala dinner honoring American Nobel laureates. Pauling remained outspoken until his death in 1994, never having rested on his laurels.

Barbara McClintock, one of the most important figures in the history of genetics, was the first woman to win an unshared Nobel Prize in the category of physiology or medicine (1983). She chose for years not to publish her most startling observations because her ideas baffled other scientists, who either dismissed or ignored them. She never gave lectures. She didn't install a telephone in her home until a few years before her death at the age of ninety in 1992.

✳ ✳ ✳

Our dreams of flight were realized in many stages. There was the hot-air balloon that would rise up but couldn't be steered, then an ornithopter that imitated the flapping of a bird's wings. Then came the helicopter, which could go up but not forward. It was followed by a glider, a variation of a kite and an important step in the evolution of flight. The glider flew well enough and carried a man, but it had no power of its own and stayed aloft only through the vagaries of winds and thermals.

Orville and Wilbur Wright were the first men to really fly. That historic first flight was of 12 seconds' duration, covered about 120 feet, at 10 feet above the ground, at a speed of 6.8 miles per hour. It changed the history of war, transportation, and exploration.

In 1976 a Lockheed SR-71A "Blackbird" flew 2,193.2 miles per hour over a 15½-mile course. The jet was reportedly capable of attaining an altitude of nearly 100,000 feet. Astronauts, in space capsules orbiting the earth, have experienced greater speeds and heights than this. Outer space is where such speeds are necessary and belong. Here on earth our private aircraft and commercial airliners collide in our crowded skies. The noise made by supersonic transports abuses our ears and nerves, and damages our buildings. Their fuels pollute our air. We are left with historian Charles A. Beard's disquieting notion: "A fool is still a fool whether he travels four miles an hour in an ox-cart or four hundred in an airplane. Wisdom is not measured by speed."

INSPIRED PROPHETS/BOLD VISIONARIES • 54–55

The freed slaves (at least the males) became full-fledged citizens of the United States and legal voters when the Thirteenth, Fourteenth, and Fifteenth Amendments to the Constitution were ratified, but they were powerless voters, robbed of many of their rights by local laws and mob action. And when the Supreme Court ruled that "separate but equal" schools and public facilities were constitutional (1896), it declared, in effect, that blacks were free but not equal.

A recurring theme in the history of America (and in this book) is that rights are not won on paper. They are won by people who make their voices heard, who are willing to sacrifice their personal comforts to accomplish the fulfillment of their beliefs. More often than not, this sacrifice requires not only courage but violence as well.

In the mid-twentieth century it took a new generation of visionaries—equally courageous—to revive the Bill of Rights and the freedoms it guarantees to all Americans and to accomplish this revival by peaceful means.

Active militancy need not be violent. Passive resistance is active militancy, and so is peaceful public demonstration. It was Martin Luther King, Jr., who changed the tactics in the battle for civil rights and led the way to substantial victories. He believed that strong people can stand up for their rights without hitting back, and that love is the greatest power in the world. Even Malcolm X, perhaps the most alienated and radical of all contemporary black leaders, came around to the martyred King's way of thinking—that what is most needed is forbearance and compassion.

✳ ✳ ✳

R. Buckminster Fuller was not a modest man. He cheerfully described himself as an "engineer, inventor, mathematician, cartographer, philosopher, poet, cosmogonist, comprehensive designer and choreographer." For years he was dismissed as a kind of crackpot, but actually he was a true original. He thought in terms of global rather than national self-improvement and had projects for turning our attention away from war and toward ultimate cooperation with the rest of the world.

Fuller used an inventory of international resources in designing his plans to save the world from itself; he believed that through technology people could create miracles to improve their environment and that survival was only possible if we organized our society with the disciplined design of a space capsule. He thought of the world as a large mechanical device, and he wrote an *Operational Manual for Spaceship Earth* with guidelines for its periodic tune-ups.

Both Dr. King and Mr. Fuller dreamed of a better tomorrow. Both were resolute in their convictions that cooperation and compassion are the only acceptable solutions to the crucial political, racial, and economic problems of our times. Both died before they reached the goals they had set for themselves. Let us do it for them.

ACKNOWLEDGMENTS

Free Spirits/Rebel Voices

Quotes: (page 10) Henry David Thoreau, from *The Correspondence of Henry David Thoreau,* edited by Carl Bode and Walter Harding (New York: New York University Press, 1958); *(page 11)* Clarence Darrow, from *Attorney for the Damned,* edited by Arthur Weinberg (New York: Simon and Schuster, Inc., 1957).

Observations & Reflections (page 56): Clifton Daniel, editor in chief. *Chronicle of the 20th Century* (Mount Kisco, N.Y.: Chronicle Publications, 1987), p. 327.

Pilgrims and Puritans/Quakers and Shakers

Quotes: (page 12) William Bradford, from "History of Plymouth Plantation 1606–1646," quoted in *A Documentary History of the American People,* by Avery Craven, Walter Johnson, and F. Roger Dunn (Boston, Mass.: Ginn and Company, 1951); *(page 13)* William Penn, from "A Further Account of the Province of Pennsylvania 1685," quoted in *A Documentary History of the American People.*

Observations & Reflections (page 56): William K. Sanford, quoted in *Recapturing Wisdoms' Valley,* by Dorothy M. Filley (Albany, N.Y.: Albany Institute of History and Art, 1975), p. v.

Maverick Ministers/Guiding Lights

Quotes: (page 14) William James, from *Varieties of Religious Experience: A Study in Human Nature* (New York: The Modern Library, Inc., 1902); *(page 15)* Tracy Kidder, from *Among Schoolchildren* (New York: Avon Books, 1989).

Observations & Reflections (pages 56–57): Will and Ariel Durant, *Religion and History* (New York: Simon and Schuster, Inc., 1968), p. 49; John Dewey, from *The School and Society,* reprinted in *A Documentary History of the American People,* by Avery Craven, Walter Johnson, and F. Roger Dunn (Boston, Mass.: Ginn and Company, 1951), p. 570; Tracy Kidder, *Among Schoolchildren,* pp. 300–301.

The Impassioned Fights for Freedom and Equal Rights

Quotes: (page 16) John Brown, quoted in *Walden and Other Writings of Henry David Thoreau,* by Henry David Thoreau, edited by Brooks Atkinson (New York: The Modern Library, Inc., 1950); *(page 17)* Susan B. Anthony, quoted in *Women of Courage,* by Dorothy Nathan (New York: Random House, Inc., 1964).

Observations & Reflections (page 57): John Brown, quoted in "Verdicts of History III: The Trial of John Brown," by Thomas J. Fleming, *American Heritage,* August 1967, p. 100 .

Warriors and Patriots

Quote: (pages 18–19) Thomas Paine, quoted in *America, I Love You,* compiled by Peter Potter (New Canaan, Conn.: William Mulvey, Inc., 1986).

Observations & Reflections (page 57): Robert E. Lee, quoted in *Historic Homes of America,* by James Tackach (New York: Random House, Inc., 1990), p. 112.

Pictorial Historians/The Fourth Estate

Quotes: (page 20) Alfred Stieglitz, quoted in *Aperture Masters of Photography,* vol. 6, *Alfred Stieglitz,* by Dorothy Newman (New York: Aperture Foundation, Inc., 1989); *(page 21)* Thomas Jefferson, from a letter to Colonel Edward Carrington, 1787.

Observations & Reflections (page 57): Oliver Wendell Holmes, quoted in *The Camera Opens Its Eye on America,* by D. Jay Culver, *American Heritage,* December 1956, p. 49; Mathew Brady, quoted in *The Civil War: An Illustrated History,* by Geoffrey C. Ward with Ric Burns and Ken Burns (New York: Alfred A. Knopf, Inc., 1991), p. 77; Horace Greeley and Abraham Lincoln, quoted in "The Life and Death of a Great Newspaper," by Fred C. Shapiro, *American Heritage,* October 1967, pp. 98, 102.

The Magnetic West: Pathfinders, Settlers, and Image Makers

Quote: (pages 22–23) Frederick Jackson Turner, quoted in "How the Frontier Shaped the American Character," by Ray Allen Billington, *American Heritage,* April 1958, p. 6.

Radical Reformers and Humanitarians

Quotes: (page 24) Henry Bergh, quoted in "The Great Meddler," by Gerald Carson, *American Heritage,* December 1967; *(page 25)* Margaret Sanger, quoted in *Woman of Valor: Margaret Sanger and the Birth Control Movement in America,* by Ellen Chesler (New York: Simon and Schuster, Inc., 1992).

Mega-Millionaires: Industrialists, Financiers, and Robber Barons

Quotes: (page 26) Peter Cooper, quoted in "The Honest Man," by Peter Lyon, *American Heritage,* February 1959; *(page 27)* John D. Rockefeller, Cornelius Vanderbilt, and J. P. Morgan, quoted in *The Great Americana Scrap Book,* edited by George Hornby (New York: Crown Publishers, Inc., 1985).

The Wobblies and the Miners: Shock Troops of the AFL-CIO

Quote: (pages 28–29) Eugene V. Debs, quoted in *The Great Americana Scrap Book,* edited by George Hornby (New York: Crown Publishers, Inc., 1985).

The Pastoral Protectors: Naturalists and Ecologists

Quotes: (page 30) Theodore Roosevelt, quoted in *The LIFE History of the United States,* vol. 9, *1901–1917: The Progressive Era,* by Ernest R. May and the editors of

Time-Life Books (Alexandria, Va.: Time-Life Books, Inc., 1980 rev. ed.); *(page 31)* Carl Sagan, from *Cosmos* (New York: Random House, Inc., 1980).

Observations & Reflections (page 58): Rachel Carson, from *Silent Spring* (Boston: Houghton Mifflin Co., 1962); Grace Paley, quoted in *Reweaving the World: The Emergence of Ecofeminism,* edited by Irene Diamond and Gloria Feman Orenstein (San Francisco: Sierra Club Books, 1990).

Worker in the Vineyard/Eccentric Autocrat

Quotes: (page 32) Peter Mathiessen, from *The New Yorker,* May 17, 1993; *(page 33)* Edmund Wilson, from *The Portable Edmund Wilson,* edited by Lewis M. Dabney (New York: Viking Press, Inc., 1983).

Observations & Reflections (pages 58–59): Quoted in *The New Yorker,* May 17, 1993, p. 82; Will Rogers, quoted in *The LIFE History of the United States,* vol. 10, *1917–1932: Boom and Bust,* by Ernest R. May and the editors of Time-Life Books (Alexandria, Va.: Time-Life Books, Inc., 1980 rev. ed.), p. 70.

Expatriates: Americans Abroad

Quotes: (page 34) James Baldwin, from *Nobody Knows My Name: More Notes of a Native Son* (New York: Dell Publishing Co., 1962); *(page 35)* Gertrude Stein, quoted in *America, I Love You,* compiled by Peter Potter (New Canaan, Conn.: William Mulvey, Inc., 1986).

Observations & Reflections (page 59): Henry James, quoted in "Americans Abroad," by Richard Gilman, *American Heritage,* October 1961, pp. 9, 18.

Writers: Fiction, History, Essays, Plays, and Criticism

Quote: (pages 36–37) William Faulkner, from *Writers at Work: The Paris Review Interviews,* edited by Malcolm Cowley (New York: Viking Press, Inc., 1961).

Poets/Poets of Motion

Quotes: (page 38) John Ciardi, from "The Act of Language," quoted in *Adventures of the Mind from The Saturday Evening Post,* edited by Richard Thruelsen and John Kobler (New York: Alfred A. Knopf, Inc., 1961); *(page 39)* Agnes de Mille, from *The Book of the Dance* (New York: Golden Press, 1963).

American Architects: The Shapes of Democracy

Quotes: (page 40) Louis Sullivan, from *Architecture, Ambition and Americans: A Social History of American Architecture,* by Wayne Andrews (New York: The Free Press, 1964); *(page 41)* Frank Lloyd Wright, from *Architecture, Ambition and Americans: A Social History of American Architecture.*

The Visual Artists

Quotes: (page 42) John K. Howat, from *The Hudson River and Its Painters* (New York: Viking Press, Inc., 1972); also John Steuart Curry's *Tornado Over Kansas:* Hackley Picture Fund, Muskegon Museum of Art, Muskegon, Mich.; *(page 43)* Susan Sontag, from *Against Interpretation, and Other Essays* (New York: Dell Publishing Co., 1969).

The Enduring Icons: Entertainers, Impresarios, and Superstars

Quote: (pages 44–45) Thomas Alva Edison, quoted in *The LIFE History of the United States,* vol. 9, *1901–1917: The Progressive Era,* by Ernest R. May and the editors of Time-Life Books (Alexandria, Va.: Time-Life Books, Inc., 1980 rev. ed.).

Composers, Classy Tunesmiths, and All That Jazz

Quotes: (page 46) Leonard Bernstein, from *The Joy of Music* (New York: Simon and Schuster, Inc., 1959); *(page 47)* Thelonius Monk, quoted in *Chronicle of the 20th Century,* edited by Clifton Daniel (Mount Kisco, N.Y.: Chronicle Publications, 1987).

Observations & Reflections (pages 59–60): Luther Henderson, quoted in "Reconstructing Jelly Through His Music," by Sheila Rule, *New York Times Large Type Weekly,* July 6, 1992, p. 33.

The Great National Pastime: Pacesetters and Groundbreakers

Quotes: (page 48) Donald Hall, from *Fathers Playing Catch with Sons: Essays on Sport, Mostly Baseball* (Berkeley, Calif.: North Point Press, 1985); *(page 49)* A. Bartlett Giamatti, from "The Green Fields of the Mind," *Yale Alumni Magazine,* November 1977.

Observations & Reflections (page 60): Geoffrey C. Ward and Ken Burns, from *Baseball: An Illustrated History* (New York: Alfred A. Knopf, Inc., 1994); Happy Chandler and Ford Frick, quoted in *The Associated Press Pictorial History of Baseball,* by Hal Bock (New York: JG Press, 1994), p. 94.

Scoundrels and Thieves/Villains and Rogues

Quotes: (page 50) Sheriff Pat Garrity, quoted in *The Great Americana Scrap Book,* edited by George Hornby (New York: Crown Publishers, Inc., 1985); *(page 51)* Al Capone, quoted in *This Fabulous Century,* vol. 3, *America 1920–1930: Racketeering Comes of Age,* by the editors of Time-Life Books (Alexandria, Va.: Time-Life Books, Inc., 1969); *The LIFE History of the United States,* vol. 10, *1917–1932: Boom and Bust,* by Ernest R. May and the editors of Time-Life Books (Alexandria, Va.: Time-Life Books, Inc., 1980 rev. ed.); and *The Great Americana Scrap Book,* edited by George Hornby (New York: Crown Publishers, Inc., 1985).

Inventing the Future: The Individual Genius

Quotes: (page 52) Mark Kac, quoted in *Genius: The Life and Science of Richard Feynman,* by James Gleick (New York: Pantheon Books, 1992); *(page 53)* Mitchell

Wilson, from *American Science and Invention: A Pictorial History* (New York: Simon and Schuster, Inc., 1954).

Observations & Reflections (page 60): Charles A. Beard, quoted in the *Indiana Magazine of History,* March 1959, reprinted in *American Heritage,* August 1959, p. 101.

Inspired Prophets/Bold Visionaries

Quotes: (page 54) Martin Luther King, Jr., source unknown; *(page 55)* R. Buckminster Fuller, from *Ideas and Integrities: A Spontaneous Autobiographical Disclosure,* edited by Robert W. Marks (New York: Collier Books, 1963).

Registered trademarks (and the owners of those marks) that appear in this book include: Academy Awards (Academy of Motion Picture Arts and Sciences); American Red Cross (American Red Cross); Andy Warhol (Executor of Andy Warhol Estate); Raggedy Ann (Macmillan, Inc.); Bing Crosby (HLC Properties, Ltd.); Blue Note (Capitol Records, Inc.); the Bobbsey Twins (Simon and Schuster, Inc.); Brooklyn Dodgers (Los Angeles Dodgers, Inc.); Charlie Chaplin (Bubbles Incorporated, S.A.); Columbia (Sony Music Entertainment, Inc.); Disneyland (The Walt Disney Company); Dr. Seuss (Dr. Seuss Enterprises, L.P.); Elvis Presley (Elvis Presley Enterprises, Inc.); Graceland (Elvis Presley Enterprises, Inc.); Greta Garbo (Harriet Brown & Co., Inc.); Groucho Marx (Groucho Marx Productions, Inc.); the Ivy League (Council of Ivy Group Presidents); James Dean (Trustees of James Dean Foundation); Jim Henson (Jim Henson Productions, Inc.); Kentucky Derby (Churchill Downs Incorporated); Keystone Kops (Keystone Kops); Lassie (Palladium Limited Partnership); Little Orphan Annie (Tribune Media Services, Inc.); Malcolm X (Betty Shabazz); Marilyn Monroe (Administratrix, C.T.A. of the Estate of Marilyn Monroe); Mickey Mouse (The Walt Disney Company); *The Muppets* (Jim Henson Productions, Inc.); New York Yankees (New York Yankees Partnership); Okeh (Sony Music Entertainment, Inc.); Radio City Music Hall (Rockefeller Group, Inc.); RCA Dog Logo (General Electric Company); RCA Victor (General Electric Company); Rin Tin Tin (Daphne Hereford); *The Saturday Evening Post* (The Benjamin Franklin Library & Medical Society); Sesame Street (Children's Television Workshop); Tall Ships (The American Sail Training Association); W. C. Fields (W. C. Fields Productions, Inc.); Walt Disney (The Walt Disney Company); Walt Disney World (The Walt Disney Company); Watergate (Watergate Hotel Partners, L. P.)

SELECTED BIBLIOGRAPHY

Andrews, Wayne. *Architecture, Ambition and Americans: A Social History of American Architecture.* New York: The Free Press, 1964.

Bernstein, Leonard. *The Joy of Music.* New York: Simon and Schuster, Inc., 1959.

Blum, Daniel. *A Pictorial History of the Silent Screen.* New York: Grosset & Dunlap, 1953.

Bock, Hal. *The Associated Press Pictorial History of Baseball,* rev. ed. New York: JG Press, 1994.

Boswell, Peyton, Jr. *Modern American Painting.* New York: Dodd, Mead & Company, 1940.

Bowen, Ezra, series ed., and the editors of Time-Life Books. *This Fabulous Century* (various vols.). Alexandria, Va.: Time-Life Books, Inc., 1969.

Bridgwater, William, and Seymour Kurtz, eds. *The Columbia Encyclopedia,* 3d ed. New York: Columbia University Press, 1963.

Brooks, Van Wyck, and Otto L. Bettmann. *Our Literary Heritage: A Pictorial History of the Writer in America.* New York: E. P. Dutton & Company, Inc., 1956.

Catton, Bruce, through Richard F. Snow, eds. *American Heritage* (numerous issues from 1956–1993). New York: American Heritage Publishing Co.

Cirker, Hayward, Blanche Cirker, and the staff of Dover Publications, Inc. *Dictionary of American Portraits.* New York: Dover Publications, Inc., 1967.

Coit, Margaret L., and the editors of Time-Life Books. *The LIFE History of the United States,* vol. 3, *1789–1829: The Growing Years.* New York: Time-Life Books, Inc., 1974 rev. ed.

Craven, Avery, Walter Johnson, and F. Roger Dunn. *A Documentary History of the American People.* Boston, Mass.: Ginn and Company, 1951.

Daniel, Clifton, ed. in chief. *Chronicle of the 20th Century.* Mount Kisco, N.Y.: Chronicle Publications, 1987.

de Mille, Agnes. *The Book of the Dance.* New York: Golden Press, 1963.

Durant, Will, and Ariel Durant. *The Lessons of History.* New York: Simon and Schuster, Inc., 1968.

Geldzahler, Henry. *New York Painting and Sculpture: 1940–1970.* New York: E. P. Dutton & Company, Inc., 1969.

Hornby, George, ed. *The Great Americana Scrap Book.* New York: Crown Publishers, Inc., 1985.

Levy, Elizabeth, and Tad Richards. *Struggle and Lose, Struggle and Win: The United Mine Workers.* New York: Four Winds Press, 1977.

May, Ernest R., and the editors of Time-Life Books. *The LIFE History of the United States,* vol. 10, *1917–1932: Boom and Bust.* Alexandria, Va.: Time-Life Books, Inc., 1980 rev. ed.

Schoener, Allen, ed. *Harlem on My Mind: Cultural Capital of Black America 1900–1968.* New York: Random House, Inc., 1968.

Williams, Trevor I. *Science: A History of Discovery in the Twentieth Century.* Oxford, England: Oxford University Press, 1990.

Wilson, Mitchell. *American Science and Invention: A Pictorial History.* New York: Simon and Schuster, Inc., 1954.